Instructional Design for the Corporate Trainer

Instructional Design for the Corporate Trainer

A Handbook on the Science of Training

Dan Chauncey

Writers Club Press

San Jose New York Lincoln Shanghai

Instructional Design for the Corporate Trainer
A Handbook on the Science of Training

Writers Club Press
an imprint of iUniverse, Inc.

For information address:
iUniverse, Inc.
5220 S. 16th St., Suite 200
Lincoln, NE 68512
www.iuniverse.com

ISBN: 0-595-22783-X

Printed in the United States of America

Life is made up of an infinite number of choices and each one is dependent on the decisions made in the preceding choices. I believe that the level of impact grows exponentially the farther it gets from those preceding choices. In other words, a choice made yesterday affects the outcomes for today. A choice made almost thirty years ago has affected an immeasurable number of outcomes. As I grow older, and hopefully wiser, I realize that the choice (assuming I actually had a choice and it was not pre-ordained somehow) to marry my wife is the one that has resulted in virtually everything wonderful in my life.

I would like to dedicate this book to my wife Wanda. For the past twenty-seven years she has put up with more annoying idiosyncrasies than any one person should be subjected to in a dozen lifetimes; yet is always there when I need her, even when I don't know I need her.

CONTENTS

FOREWORD

So, you are—or are studying to be—a trainer. How is it that you chose this profession? I'll bet when you were twelve and your teacher asked, "What do you want to be when you grow up?" you didn't say, "A trainer."

So where do trainers come from? Some of us were promoted into the role of trainer because we were the subject matter experts—and our boss believed that technical knowledge was the key to being a great trainer. Some of today's trainers were public school teachers or military instructors to whom training appeared to be a natural career transition. Others 'fell' into the profession—whether through an intentional career change, taking on a training project during a layoff, or just happening to get into the profession by answering a classified ad.

If any of these stories sound like your own, know that you are not alone. Trainers come to the profession in many ways…and until recently most arrived with little formal education or training on how adults learn. It doesn't take long before a new trainer realizes that technical knowledge, the ability to create a PowerPoint presentation, or great public speaking skills alone aren't enough to be a trainer.

What it takes is a clear understanding and prudent application of the art and the science of training.

The science of training is as complex as the human brain and cannot be acquired through on-the-job experience. This is why I found Dan Chauncey's book, *Instructional Design for the Corporate Trainer*, a valuable tool for adult learning professionals. This book revealed the science behind the successful things I was doing purely through intuition (and luck) and showed me how I can make the results of my training programs even more powerful and laser focused.

Instructional Design for the Corporate Trainer builds the foundation of adult learning. In these pages Dan provides sound research, examples of application, and then challenges us to:

- Write objectives based on the level of learning desired
- Organize the learning event in a logical fashion
- Select teaching methods that deliver the objective
- Create a real lesson plan so that the learning can be reproduced, measured, and revised as needed
- …And much more

These topics may sound old fashioned and parochial to you. No matter how they sound, know that these concepts and processes work! You owe it to yourself—and your students—to use *Instructional Design for the Corporate Trainer* as your guide to designing curriculum that delivers real performance improvement.

Yours in learning,

Cindy Stynchula
The Art of Training©
Owner, Stynchula & Associates
www.stynchula.com
cindy@stynchula.com

PREFACE

Learning means many things to many people. To some, learning is simply a change in behavior as a result of experience; to others, it is something more difficult to see and measure which involves changing thought processes or attitudes. We learn to name objects as children and solve complex problems as adults. We learn attitudes and values. We even learn to learn by improving study skills. But, how do we explain learning? Can any one method or theory explain how we have learned all of what we can do, what we know, and why our attitudes and values are what they are? More importantly, what do we need to know about learning theory to be effective educators?

Learning is popularly defined as a change in behavior based on instruction. If this is true, then after receiving instruction, students should behave differently than before receiving it. Moreover, if we have used student-centered objectives, that behavior will be exactly what we predicted it would be. We will be able to demonstrate our students' success in learning by having them demonstrate the same physical or mental skill described in the objective.

Since the 1950's there has been a movement to promote student-centered instruction through the use of appropriate objectives. One would think that student-centered objectives, which describe learning in terms of student outcomes versus instructor inputs, would be increasing. With the continued push for accountability in expenditures and the need to improve overall quality, one would think the trend toward student-centered instruction would be the norm. I have found that this is not true.

This book will provide training professionals with an academic foundation as well as a structured approach for developing training programs that facilitate student retention. Training programs with clearly defined objectives. Training programs that will provide a means to measure success. Training programs that can demonstrate their cost effectiveness.

ACKNOWLEDGEMENTS

This section is difficult for me to write. I know that many people have influenced my style and ideas, as well as the materials in this book. I hesitate to begin listing them because I know I'll leave someone out. First, let me cite the person who gave me my first real opportunity to be involved in training: Dale Roberts. Dale makes the short list of true leaders I have met. He took chances and supported his people. Next, I would like to acknowledge Cindy Stynchula for constantly badgering me to finish this book. Without that badgering, I don't know if I would have had the perseverance to get it done.

Finally, I want to acknowledge an institution, the United States Air Force. I went into the Air Force a high school graduate (barely) and got the chance to grow, learn, and succeed. While, the primary mission of the Air Force is to fly planes; they recognize that an outstanding training program is essential to meeting that mission. I was proud to be a small part of that training during my tenure. I came to understand that a structured approach is the only way to ensure that educational objectives are met. Much of the approach I posit in this book comes directly from the way I learned it at the Air Force Academic Instructor Course at Maxwell AFB, AL.

INTRODUCTION

After almost twenty-five years participating in and observing the practice of corporate training and development I have come to a sobering conclusion. The science of training is dying. Arising in its place is the art of presenting. Don't get me wrong; presentation is an important facet of the instructional process. To me, it is much like the siding and trim on a house. It is essential for the appearance, durability, and strength of the structure. But to focus attention on this at the detriment of the foundation will result in fundamental flaws in the structure. The same is true for training.

Training can be separated into two processes: instructional or training design and training delivery. Observing training in the "real world" (wherever that may be), I continue to be amazed at the prevalence of practitioners who place the majority of their efforts on the delivery of the training to the detriment of the design process. I label these two distinct processes as the *"science of training"* (instructional design) and the *"art of training"* (training delivery)

How can one adequately train people in a manner that enables retention without first clearly articulating what the student should retain? To this end, I have prepared what I believe is a practical book for the training professional. My intent is to facilitate understanding the underlying theories that make training successful, as well as provide a methodology that will make your training more effective.

Test my observations. Think about the last training session you attended. Think about the presentation. Was there a theme? Perhaps it may have been as obvious the entire program being based on a trip. The introductory part of the session may have been a "welcome aboard" address by the "ship's captain" or "activities director". It may have been as subtle as using standard backgrounds on the computerized slide show or overhead transparencies.

Next, ask yourself what were the objectives of that same session. I realize that most of us can discern some high level objectives from any session we attend; but were the specific outcomes clear to you? More importantly, can you say with any degree of certainty that they were clear to the trainer?

Take a different approach at the next session you attend. After the session, ask the trainer what the learning objectives for the session were. Listen carefully and write them down. Ask yourself if they were true objectives or something as simple as a general idea of what the trainer wanted the student to learn?

It is important that each reader understand that my intent is for each of you to become practitioners in the science of training. Hopefully the majority of you will leave this book with a better understanding of the science of training and will transform that knowledge into better training products for your students. The instructional design process presented in this book is shown below.

Instructional Design Checklist

☐ Develop level of learning objectives (both cognitive and affective if applicable).

☐ Develop sufficient samples of behavior to effective gauge attainment of learning objectives.

☐ Conduct subject matter research (not covered in this book).

☐ Determine most effective teaching method(s).

☐ Determine most effective organization pattern(s).

☐ Develop Lesson Plan (including a detailed strategy statement).

☐ Develop Teaching Plan.

☐ Teach the lesson.

Note: At any point in the design process resource availability may force you to adjust your level of learning or teaching method.

Part I

ADULT LEARNING THEORY

I wanted to begin this book with a brief introduction to Adult Learning Theory or Andragogy. Some of the following comments and the second chapter of the book may be widely disagreed with by education experts and researchers. While I do not profess to be a researcher like many of those referred to in this book, I do believe that, as a practitioner, my thoughts and beliefs are valid. My observations are that when asked about adult learning, most practitioners will address two issues:

- Learning must be relevant to the student. They need to see a need for the knowledge or skill, and

- Leaning must be "just in time." They student sees that the material can be applied within a short period of time following the learning experience.

These two widely accepted concepts are nothing more than truisms to me. I believe they apply to all learners, regardless of age. The approach to delivering the materials may differ, but the premise remains the same. How many of us asked, "When will I use American History in the real world?" when we were in school? We still learned it, but did we all retain it?

Was our level of retention affected by how that question was answered? We may have had a teacher who said that we might never need it, but we sure had to know it for next Friday's test. Or, we may have had a teacher who found a way to answer and make it relevant to our perception of the "real world". I will talk about andragogy (adult learning) in the first chapter. I will discuss my thoughts, which may differ from the mainstream, in the second chapter.

CHAPTER 1

Theory of Andragogy

Malcolm Knowles' theory of andragogy is an attempt to develop a theory specifically for adult learning. Knowles emphasizes that adults are self-directed and expect to take responsibility for decisions. Adult learning programs must accommodate this fundamental aspect.

Andragogy makes the following assumptions about the design of learning:

- Adults need to know why they need to learn something,
- Adults need to learn experientially,
- Adults approach learning as problem-solving, and
- Adults learn best when the topic is of immediate value.

In practical terms, andragogy means that instruction for adults needs to focus more on the process and less on the content being taught. Strategies such as case studies, role-playing, simulations, and self-evaluation are most useful. Instructors adopt a role of facilitator or resource rather than lecturer or grader.

CHAPTER 2

Why Are Adults Different?

This chapter is simply intended to make you think. Many of you may disagree. My premise may shake the very foundation that you have been taught for years: That teaching adults is different. It seems as though we (training practitioners) have accepted this as a given and moved forward blindly reciting the mantra:

…Adults are different

…Adults are different

…Adults are different

But how many of us have asked how are they different? Take a couple of minutes to think about what makes teaching adults different than teaching children and then apply that very rule to children.

- Adults need to know why they need to learn something.

    How many times have you tried to explain something to children and they wouldn't listen. How did you get their attention? My experience is that I had to capture their attention by telling them why they should listen.

- Adults need to learn experientially.

    Don't children learn better if you make a game out of it? The best classes in my primary education were when the teachers made it participative. I can still remember some of the lessons from eighth grade American History. Every Thursday that year we played a game similar to Jeopardy.

- Adults approach learning as problem solving.

  Although we all hated them, why are word problems used so much in elementary education? Why couldn't the lesson of how Columbus obtained funding for his journey to the new world be taught as a series of questions? Isn't Socratic teaching a form of problem solving?

  - Adults learn best when the topic is of immediate value.

    I go back to the example cited earlier in this book: How many times did we ask when will I use geometry, trigonometry, etc. in the real world? The better that was explained, the better I learned. How about you?

  - Instruction should be task-oriented instead of memorization—learning activities should be in the context of common tasks to be performed.

    Don't children learn better with hands-on? Think back to the various courses you took as a child. Which ones were easier; those that required memorization or those that allowed you to "do it?"

  - Instruction should allow learners to discover things for themselves, providing guidance and help when mistakes are made.

    Was it more gratifying for you as a child to discover things for yourself? How many times have you seen the light come on in a child's eye when they finally figured out how to accomplish something?

I know there are many who will say that this view of andragogy is too narrow and simplistic. That may well be so, however, it goes to the point of this entire book. The bottom line is that the approach is dependent on what the objective of the lesson is. It doesn't matter if it is child or adult, you need to begin with an end in mind—figure out where you want the student to go before you decide how to get them there.

Part II

PSYCHOLOGY OF LEARNING

Many theories try to explain how we learn, but psychologists and educators do not totally agree on any one of them. Most agree, however, that learning is best explained by some mix two psychological philosophies: behaviorism or cognitive psychology.

A third concept is motivation. While not necessarily a psychological philosophy of its own, it is a primary driver in both behaviorism and cognitive psychology.

CHAPTER 3

Behaviorism

We know that all animals can learn. Many psychologists and educators believe that all animals, including humans, learn in about the same way. Behaviorists believe that we learn by having our behavior reinforced, and that our behavior can be shaped or controlled by someone else. In the classroom, the "someone else" is the instructor.

If what we do as students is positively reinforced, we will learn to do it better and more often. If we get no reinforcement or are punished for something we do, we tend to stop doing it. And, in general, it is better to get people to learn what we want them to learn by providing positive rewards than by punishing them.

The technical features of behaviorism are far more complex than this simple explanation. Those who need high-level understanding of behaviorism and its principles, especially authors of programmed instruction and other self-paced learning materials, should read the works of B. F. Skinner and J. G. Holland. As classroom instructors we need to realize the importance of controlling learning experiences by manipulating the classroom environment (stimuli), which gives our students a chance to behave or perform (respond) in the way that we desire and can reward (reinforce).

Behaviorism certainly explains the way our students learn much of what we teach. We need to be aware of the importance of stimulus, response, and reinforcement as they affect our classrooms. These are important concepts to consider as we plan, deliver, and evaluate instruction.

CHAPTER 4

Cognitive Psychology

Much of psychological thinking and experimentation today falls into the general category of cognitive psychology. Unlike the behaviorists, the cognitive psychologists are very concerned about what is going on inside the learner. Learning is not just a change in behavior; it is a change in the way a student thinks, understands, or feels.

Motivation, generalizing, insight, and discovery are significant concepts to cognitive theorists. While all learning theories hold that instructors have the responsibility to set up an environment that motivates students, cognitive theorists believe that instructors we must plan learning experiences that allow students to go beyond simple recall and cause students to gain an understanding of what they study.

Like the behaviorists, the cognitive psychologists acknowledge the importance of reinforcing behavior and measuring changes. Positive reinforcement is important when we are concerned with cognitive concepts such as knowledge and understanding. We still need to measure behavior, however, because it is the only way we can get a clue about what the student understands. While students may be able to do much more with what we teach than we are able to test, we have to measure what we can. There will be errors in measurement as we try to measure understanding, but since understanding cannot be measured directly we have little choice. Since we want to quantify learning, we have to measure and interpret behavior.

Both the behavioral and cognitive approaches are useful theories for instructors. We can see from the two brief descriptions above that each theory can contribute to the way we plan, deliver, and evaluate instruction. Perhaps the best approach to planning and managing instruction is an approach that includes features of each major theory. The approach that retains the notion of cognitive learning while measuring behavioral outcomes seems to be the most workable. We can plan for low or high order cognitive outcomes and determine if these outcomes have been achieved by measuring and interpreting behavior. We often say that students really understand something because they can do this or that. We can plan for cognitive learning, but we must use behavioral evidence of learning.

CHAPTER 5

Motivation

Motivation is a pivotal concept in the instructional process. It is closely related to arousal, attention, anxiety, and feedback/reinforcement. For example, a person needs to be motivated enough to pay attention while learning; anxiety can decrease our motivation to learn. Receiving a reward or feedback for an action usually increases the likelihood that the action will be repeated. In most forms of behavioral theory, motivation was strictly a function of primary drives such as hunger, sex, sleep, or comfort. According to Clark L. Hull's drive reduction theory, learning reduces drives and therefore motivation is essential to learning. The degree of the learning achieved can be manipulated by the strength of the drive and its underlying motivation.

In cognitive theory, motivation serves to create intentions and goal-seeking acts. One well-developed area of research highly relevant to learning is achievement motivation. Motivation to achieve is a function of the individual's desire for success, the expectancy of success, and the incentives provided. Studies show that in general people prefer tasks of intermediate difficulty. In addition, students with a high need to achieve tend to obtain better grades in courses which they perceive as highly relevant to their goals.

John C. Malone presented a theoretical framework for intrinsic motivation. According to Malone, intrinsically motivating activities provide learners with a broad range of challenge, concrete feedback, and clear-cut criteria for performance. Fred S. Keller presents an instructional design model for motivation that is based upon a number of other theories. His model suggests a design strategy that encompasses four components of motivation: arousing interest, creating relevance, developing an expectancy of success, and producing satisfaction through intrinsic/extrinsic rewards.

Part III

FOUNDATIONS OF LEARNING

When we're deciding what to teach and how we're going to measure success it isn't enough to simply determine who our students are, what they will need to know, or how we will present the material to them. When the planning stops there, we've failed to consider the most important element of the instructional design process; what our students will be able to do once they have received and processed the information we present.

It doesn't necessarily follow that what we present in class is what the student will learn. This mistaken belief has driven our public educational system for years. For when we break the teaching process down into its basic elements we realize that, just as in any form of human communication, in the teaching-learning relationship there is always the possibility of transmitting false messages or receiving misunderstood symbols. Without effective and meaningful feedback to both the instructor and the student, the resultant problems go undetected and uncorrected.

This book attacks the assumption that, in order to develop effective lessons, it is enough to determine what the instructor must do in the classroom. Education is a shared process. Both the student and the instructor have certain responsibilities and expectations. But it stresses the primacy of the instructor's responsibility to develop lessons that bridge the gap between instructor and student responsibilities. I propose that writing objectives that focus on the abilities we want the student to display after having received the instruction can bridge this gap. With student-centered objectives, instructors will be better able to plan teaching activities designed to efficiently impart and display the knowledge they want the students to learn.

Several approaches for planning instruction exist which combine cognitive concepts and behavioral evidence of learning. I believe that the taxonomies, or hierarchies, of learning of Drs. Benjamin Bloom and D. R. Krathwohl provide a vehicle for writing desired outcomes and measuring behavior.

By using these taxonomies you can select distinct levels of learning and specify measurable behaviors that will give a reasonable evidence of learning at the respective levels of learning. The approach to using these taxonomies will be explained in considerable detail in subsequent chapters.

There are several taxonomies that deal with physical or psychomotor skills. The taxonomy developed by A. J. Harrow is generally acceptable to those who plan instruction leading to psychomotor skills. I do not address psychomotor skills in this book.

CHAPTER 6

Bloom's Cognitive Taxonomy

This taxonomy provides a means of rank ordering learning within the cognitive domain. We must pass through each of the rank orders or levels as we move to the more complex behaviors; we must have some "knowledge" in a subject area before we can "comprehend" concepts or principles in the same subject area. We must have "comprehension" of principles before we can "apply" these principles to new situations, and so on up the ladder of the taxonomy. Each of the following six levels in this rank order forms the basis for writing level of learning objectives, as well as sequencing of lessons within a block of instruction.

Levels of the Cognitive Taxonomy
• Knowledge
• Comprehension
• Application
• Analysis
• Synthesis
• Evaluation

Fig. 6.1 - Levels of the Cognitive Taxonomy

LEVELS OF THE COGNITIVE TAXONOMY

Knowledge

The recall or recognition of previously learned material (facts, theories, etc.).

At the knowledge level of this taxonomy we are asking that students recall or remember information in essentially the same form in which it was given to them. Students may receive this information from lectures, readings, programmed texts, video or audiotapes, computer-based instruction, or other means. The source of the information has no bearing on what we expect the student to be able to do to meet our knowledge-level objective. The students simply memorize and store information, which they then give back to us, essentially verbatim, when evaluated.

Comprehension

Seeing relationships, concepts, and abstractions beyond the simple remembering of material. Typically involves translating, interpreting, and estimating future trends.

At the comprehension level of this taxonomy we go beyond simple recall and attempt to attach a meaning to what is communicated. In doing so, we try to establish relationships between pieces of information in order to form concepts, principles, and generalizations. Within the comprehension level, we can establish what we might call a mini-taxonomy. Thus, after reaching the knowledge level, students must pass through all three levels of this mini-taxonomy within comprehension before they reach the application level.

Translation

First, we would expect a student to "translate" material from one form to another. As an example, we might ask students to tell us in "their own words" what something means, ask them to "paraphrase" a lengthy reading, or ask them to look at a graph or chart and tell us verbally, or in writing, what the various parts mean. We have gone a step beyond simply recalling information; we are now asking the students to give a meaning to what they have learned.

Interpret

At the second level of comprehension, we are primarily interested in students' ability to see relationships between various aspects of a communication. In order to interpret, they must first "translate" what the individual parts mean, and then see the relationship between these parts. We can see the evidence for interpretation when students perform such activities as making inferences, generalizations, and summations.

Extrapolate

At the third level of comprehension, we want our students to be able to answer the question, "What would happen if?" That is, we want them to go beyond the literal message contained in the communication and make predictions of consequences or trends. We would also expect the students to be able to tell us, with some reasonable degree of accuracy, the probability of their prediction, not statistical probability necessarily, but general probability such as "it would very likely happen" or "it's only slightly probable."

Application

The ability to use learned material in new and concrete situations, including the application of rules, methods, concepts, principles, laws, and theories.

At the application level of this taxonomy, we are asking our students to take the concepts and principles they have formed at the comprehension level and put them to use in situations new to them. For example, suppose we have just completed a block of instruction in which our students learned to comprehend several concepts of management, and one of the concepts they learned was "delegation of authority." Now, we want to evaluate their "application" of the concept. We might give them a case study of an organization in which the concept of "delegation of authority" was violated, causing problems in the organization. We would then ask them to read the scenario and give us their solutions to the problem, but we would not tell them which concept was being violated. The criteria for evaluation would then be for the students to solve the problem by applying the "delegation of authority" concept to the organization described in the case study.

Many instructors have difficulty in differentiating between the higher levels of comprehension and application, and indeed the difference can sometimes be confusing. However, if we keep the following ideas in mind, distinguishing between the two should be easier.

At the comprehension level, students are able to demonstrate the use of a principle or concept when the principle or concept is identified. At the application level, when given a problem situation, students must identify the concepts and principles involved by themselves, and then demonstrate use of the principle or concept in solving the problem.

For example, in the "delegation of authority" situation, if we tell students that the scenario involves the misuse of "delegation of authority" and then tell them to solve the problem, they are working at the comprehension level, but by not telling them which concept is being violated and by making them come to this determination by themselves, we ensure they are working at the application level.

As we have suggested, the application level of the taxonomy is the point where students first encounter the "problem-solving" process.

Application is, or should be, the level of learning that most training departments attempt to reach. Just because students "comprehend" concepts and principles, we have no guarantee that they can "apply" these concepts and principles in new situations. The opportunity for practice of "application" level of learning activities must be provided for our students before we can expect them to function at this level.

Before we leave the application level, let us be sure we are clear on an area that often presents problems to both students and instructors. The word "application", when used as a cognitive level-of-learning, is not synonymous with the meaning of the word as we use it in our everyday speech. If we put this in terms of educational objectives, the term "apply" is not necessarily synonymous with the term "be able to." We find the confusion most prevalent in dealing with skill development. Suppose we use the objective: "Be able to solve an algebraic equation for one unknown." If we think back to our high school or college algebra courses, most of us can remember how we learned to meet this type of objective. We simply memorized the rules that applied and used these rules to solve the equation. Seldom was there any effort on our part, or the teacher's, to have us comprehend the meaning behind the rule. Thus, we could solve the problem, but we were not really at the application level-of-learning. We often saw the results of this type of learning when we were asked to solve "word problems" in algebra or other types of mathematics, where we needed a comprehension of the concepts and principles involved to solve the problem.

There is a clear implication here for instructors and instructional designers. If students are expected to problem-solve or troubleshoot on the job, then they must be at the "application" level-of-learning, and, to get there, they must have satisfactorily passed through the lower levels of the taxonomy.

Analysis

The ability to break down material into its component parts so that the organizational structure may be understood, including the identification of the parts, analysis of the relationships between parts, and recognition of the organizational principles involved.

Synthesis

The ability to put parts together to form new patterns or structures, such as a unique communication (a theme or speech), a plan of operations (a research proposal), or a set of abstract relations (schemes for classifying information).

Evaluation

The ability to judge the value of material for a given purpose. Learning in this area is the highest in the cognitive hierarchy because it involves elements of all the other categories, plus conscious value judgments based on clearly defined criteria.

CHAPTER 7

Krathwohl's Affective Taxonomy

Although it is very convenient to think of the cognitive and affective domains of learning as being separate, in fact they are not. Educators have treated the domains of learning as separate entities to make it easier to conceptualize them. In reality, learning takes place and behavior is affected in more than one domain at the same time.

We can and should plan for measurable learning outcomes. Although in most cases the focus is on the cognitive or subject matter outcomes, we should not ignore the need to plan for attitude development. Attitude development is complicated and must be approached with caution, but the affective domain in still of great importance to us as instructors. We should realize our potential effect upon student attitudes. Further, we should be aware that many of the techniques for writing and measuring cognitive objectives apply to the affective domain. We may find that affective objectives are more difficult to write and that the measuring tools are less precise, but paying more systematic attention to the affective domain will improve our course.

Although most of our objectives may be cognitive, we would often like an indication of the effect our instruction has on student attitudes. Much of the affective impact of cognitive lessons is in the way instructors deal with the subject matter. If it is taught effectively, student attitudes will probably be positive. If it is taught poorly, their attitudes might well be negative.

Dr. D. R. Krathwohl and associates first presented a basic structure for attitude development in 1956. Their work provides a taxonomy that we can use to plan and classify instructional objectives. The affective taxonomy is rank ordered. Attitudes develop through five identifiable levels and a person cannot reach a level of attitude development without first attaining the level below it.

Levels of the Affective Taxonomy

- Receiving

- Responding

- Valuing

- Organizing

- Characterization

Fig. 7.1 - Levels of the Affective Taxonomy

LEVELS OF THE AFFECTIVE TAXONOMY

Receiving

The first step in any teaching effort is to get the students to receive, that is, to pay attention or listen to what is being presented. Awareness of what is being communicated is the issue at this level. Willing attention is a logical follow-on to awareness, with selective attention following that. Selective attention is important because students choose the stimulus they will attend to.

Responding

If learning is to occur, getting students simply to listen to a message is not enough. Once we are sure of being received, we want our students to do something. Responding involves some sort of action or response on the part of the student. At first, the student may respond by merely complying. Later, the student may willingly perform an action and obtain satisfaction from it. Responding behavior at a high level is reflected in what we commonly refer to as "interests," that is, those activities that bring personal satisfaction.

Valuing

As a person responds, some worth or value may be seen in what is being done. Students may come to accept, prefer, or commit themselves to an object or activity because of its perceived worth or value. When students value something, we can also say that they "appreciate it." Commonly used terms associated with valuing are "attitudes" and "appreciation."

Organization

At this level students compare, relate, and synthesize newly taught values into their own value system. Conflicts between the new material and the existing value system must be resolved because we cannot hold two strongly opposing values or attitudes at the same time. Hence, this synthesizing step must occur as part of the development of a philosophy of life, which takes place in the next level.

Characterization

At the highest affective level, the student incorporates values into a system and that system now becomes characteristic of the student. These values now are the student; they represent a student's way of life or life style. Behaviors that result from such values are considered typical for a given individual.

SUMMARY

For purposes of example, let's look at teaching the use of planning in giving effective employee feedback. Awareness is not enough, so our next step is to get the students to act on the information. At first, students plan feedback sessions because they are told to do so—simple compliance at the responding level. Willingness to respond emerges and later develops into satisfaction with responding. As students go through feedback session planning procedures, some of them will begin to see some worth or value in planning a feedback session. A plan helps them clearly state what is to be accomplished. It is a handy outline they can use in the session. Most students will begin to feel more confident with a plan available. Hence, we have obviously arrived at the valuing level of the affective taxonomy.

As experience increases, the value of counseling session planning may be assimilated into the students' value system through the process of organization. This is a phase that a person goes through to fit the new value into his or her existing structure of values. At some point in the future someone may say, "I need to provide feedback to one of my employees," and the immediate reply will be: "First, you'll have to develop a plan." This positive attitude toward feedback session planning now seems to be typical or characteristic of the student. Student behavior can then be generally predicted in terms of the value of planning. The characterization level has been achieved.

CHAPTER 8

Documenting the Level of Learning Objectives

Once the appropriate level is determined, the next step is to determine and document the level of learning objectives and samples of behavior. Every level of learning objective must contain three elements.

Requirements for Level of Learning Objectives
• **Student-centeredness**
• <u>Expectation</u>
• *Specific subject*

Fig. 8.1 – Requirements for Level of Learning Objectives

LEVEL OF LEARNING OBJECTIVES

Student-centeredness

Since the purpose of any learning objective is to express the outcome of the lesson in terms of learner behavior, this part of the level of learning objective ensures that our focus is on the word "student." This portion of the objective is written as: "The objective of this lesson is for each student to...."

Expectation

Every objective should state the level of the taxonomy (cognitive or affective) we expect our students to reach by the end of a training session or block of instruction. This portion of the objective is written as: "...know (or comprehend, apply, analyze, synthesize, evaluate, receive, respond, value, organize, characterize)..."

Specific Subject

How specific to make the subject of the lesson normally depends on two variables: The scope of the content covered by the objective and the level-of-learning. This portion of the objective may be written as: "...all twenty-six letters of the alphabet in order.

Listed below are examples of level of learning objectives for both taxonomies. Note three elements in each objective (student-centered: **bold**, expectation: <u>underlined</u>, and specific subject *italicized*).

Sample Level of Learning Objectives for the Cognitive Domain

- Knowledge: "The objective of this lesson is for each student to <u>know</u> *the six levels of learning in Bloom's Taxonomy and their sequence.*"

- Comprehension: "The objective of this lesson is for each student to <u>comprehend</u> *the role of level of learning objectives in the instructional design process.* "

- Application: "The objective of this lesson is for each student to <u>apply</u> *level of learning objectives in the instructional design process.* "

- Analysis: "The objective of this lesson is for each student to <u>analyze</u> *the role of the instructor in each of the teaching methods.* "

- Synthesis: "The objective of this lesson is for each student to <u>synthesize</u> *the cognitive and affective level of learning objectives into their instructional design.*"

- Evaluation: "The objective of this lesson is for each student to <u>evaluate</u> *the impact of affective levels of learning on the cognitive levels.*"

Fig. 8.2 – Sample Level of Learning Objectives for the Cognitive Domain

---

Sample Level of Learning Objectives for the Affective Domain

- Receiving: "The objective of this lesson is for each student to <u>receive</u> *the importance of level of learning objectives.*"

- Responding: "The objective of this lesson is for each student to <u>respond</u> *positively to the importance of documenting level of learning objectives and samples of behavior.* "

- Valuing: "The objective of this lesson is for each student to <u>value</u> *the role of the strategy as an integral part of the lesson plan.* "

- Organizing: "The objective of this lesson is for each student to <u>organize</u> *the use of level or learning objectives into their own instructional design process.* "

- Characterization: "The objective of this lesson is for each student to <u>characterize</u> *structured instructional design.*"

Fig. 8.3 – Sample Level of Learning Objectives for the Affective Domain

SAMPLES OF BEHAVIOR

We can define a sample of behavior as a statement that specifies one of several observable behaviors which students should be able to demonstrate at the end of a period or block of instruction and which gives us evidence that they have achieved our objectives. A sample of behavior objective contains three elements.

Requirements for Sample of Behavior

- Observable and measurable
- Significant evidence of achievement
- Linked to a level-of-learning

Fig. 8.4 – Requirements for Samples of Behavior

The word evidence is the key here. There may be a great many behaviors we would expect students to demonstrate to us as evidence that, for example, they comprehend a concept or principle. In fact, there would be far more ways than we could ever have time to observe and evaluate. For this reason, we list a reasonable number (a sampling) of behaviors that are as equivalent in nature as we can possibly make them. We conclude that if students can demonstrate these behaviors, they will be able to demonstrate others. This sampling procedure is the same as any other sampling procedure—the larger the sample, the greater confidence we can put in the evidence obtained.

We may accept many or just a few student behaviors as evidence of learning. The important thing for us to ensure is that any evaluation must be comprehensive enough to give reasonable assurance that what we accept as evidence gives a true representation of that knowledge. We can never completely measure some cognitive skills or attitudes. However, carefully planned samples of behavior should provide us with adequate proof of learning.

While these samples eventually become the basis for our evaluation, not all of them will be in the form of test questions. In many cases it is either not practical or not possible to test the student (one example might be a leadership class given to senior leaders within you own organization—would you want to tell your CEO that she failed the leadership test?). In these cases, the behaviors can be demonstrated by student actions during the training session. The student may not even know they are being evaluated. Another benefit of this "concurrent evaluation" is the opportunity to take corrective action on the spot. As an example, let's suppose that the lesson objective is: "The objective of this lesson is for each student to value the concept of level of learning objectives." And the sample of behavior is: "Each student will initiate a discussion supporting concept of level of learning objectives." During a break you overhear a student enter a conversation and stridently defend the reasons his organization should change their instructional design methodology. Don't you think this clearly demonstrates that the object was met?

In higher-level cognitive or affective learning the relationship between student behavior and the level of learning is not always that clear. We know we cannot directly measure understanding or attitudes, so we must decide which behaviors give us the best evidence of learning. Although there is always the danger that we may err in translating learning into behavior, it is a task we must accomplish because the value of measuring learning by its outcomes far outweighs the risk of error. Certain behavioral verbs lend themselves for use at each level of both the cognitive and affective taxonomies.

First, the verb must reflect an observable behavior. Second, there should be a good variety of verbs. Thus, if our objective was at the comprehension level and we decided to write five samples, we would not want all of our samples to specify "explain." Instead, we might have one sample using "explain," and others with "differentiate," "compare," "paraphrase," "predict," and so forth. These samples would give us a wide variety of behaviors on which to base our judgment that the student "comprehends" our objective. Listed below are some sample behavioral verbs and as well as samples of behavior for each level of learning in both the cognitive and affective domains.

Cognitive Domain

Level of Learning Objective and Samples of Behavior for the Knowledge Level

Level of Learning Objective:

The objective of this lesson is for each student to <u>know</u> the six levels of learning in Bloom's Taxonomy and their sequence.

Samples of Behavior

The student will list the levels of learning included in Bloom's Taxonomy.

The student will select the levels of learning included in Bloom's Taxonomy.

The student will match verbs with the appropriate level of learning included in Bloom's Taxonomy.

Behavioral Verb Examples:

Define	Describe
Label	List
Name	Match
Select	State
Identify	Reproduce

Fig. 8.5 – Level of Learning Objective and Samples of Behavior for the Knowledge Level

Level of Learning Objective and Samples of Behavior for the Comprehension Level

Level of Learning Objective:

The objective of this lesson is for each student to comprehend *the role of level of cognitive learning objectives in the education process.*

Samples of Behavior

The student will give examples of classes that would require student to attain the comprehension level of learning included in Bloom's Cognitive Taxonomy.

The student will explain the relevance of the levels of learning included in Bloom's Cognitive Taxonomy.

The student will distinguish between levels of learning included in Bloom's Cognitive Taxonomy.

Behavioral Verb Examples:

Convert	Defend
Summarize	Distinguish
Estimate	Paraphrase
Generalize	Relate
Give example	Explain
Infer	Extend

Fig. 8.6 – Level of Learning Objective and Samples of Behavior for the Comprehension Level

Level of Learning Objective and Samples of Behavior for the Application Level

Level of Learning Objective:

The objective of this lesson is for each student to <u>apply</u> *level of learning objectives in the instructional design process.*

Samples of Behavior

The student will demonstrate the use level of learning objectives in developing lesson plans.

The return to their workplace each student will modify their current lesson plans to include level of learning objectives.

The student will determine the appropriate level of learning based on desired student outcomes.

Behavioral Verb Examples:

Analyze	Manipulate
Use	Perform
Solve	Demonstrate
Change	Appraise
Compute	Discover
Discover	Modify
Diagram	Operate
Relate	Show

Fig. 8.7 – Level of Learning Objective and Samples of Behavior for the Application Level

Level of Learning Objective and Samples of Behavior for the Analysis Level

Level of Learning Objective:

The objective of this lesson is for each student to <u>analyze</u> *the role of the instructor in each of the teaching methods.*

Samples of Behavior

The student will weigh the alternatives associated with teaching method selection.

Upon return to their own workplace the student will establish a plan to determine the appropriateness of the teaching methods currently used in their lessons.

The student will articulate the reasons that the level of instructor knowledge varies across teaching methods.

Behavioral Verb Examples:

Adhere to	Alter
Combine	Defend
Form judgments	Identify
Integrate	Organize
Articulate	Plan
Establish	Arrange
Classify	Weigh alternatives

Fig. 8.8 – Level of Learning Objective and Samples of Behavior for the Analysis Level

Level of Learning Objective and Samples of Behavior for the Synthesis Level

Level of Learning Objective:

The objective of this lesson is for each student to <u>synthesize</u> *the cognitive and affective level of learning objectives into their own instructional design.*

Samples of Behavior

The student will propose changes to their organization's training development methodology to include cognitive and affective level of learning objectives.

The student will summarize the benefits of cognitive and affective level of learning objectives.

The student will explain how the use of level of learning objectives.

Behavioral Verb Examples:

Alter	Change behavior
Categorize	Create
Summarize	Explain
Influence	Propose
Act	Qualify
Question	Serve
Listen	Judge issues

Fig. 8.9 – Level of Learning Objective and Samples of Behavior for the Synthesis Level

Level of Learning Objective and Samples of Behavior for the Evaluation Level

Level of Learning Objective:

The objective of this lesson is for each student to <u>evaluate</u> *the impact of affective levels of learning on the cognitive levels.*

Samples of Behavior

The student will support the benefits of using both cognitive and affective level of learning objectives.

The student will evaluate the benefits of using both cognitive and affective level of learning objectives.

The student will summarize the impact of using both cognitive and affective level of learning objectives.

Behavioral Verb Examples:

Compare	Discriminate
Infer	Interpret
Relate	Evaluate
Support	Explain
Appraise	Contrast
Decide	Conclude
Criticize	Summarize

Fig. 8.10 – Level of Learning Objective and Samples of Behavior for the Evaluation Level

Affective Domain

Level of Learning Objective and Samples of Behavior for the Receiving Level

Level of Learning Objective:

The objective of this lesson is for each student to <u>receive</u> *the importance of level of learning objectives.*

Samples of Behavior

The student will ask pertinent questions regarding level of learning objectives.

The student will listen attentively during the classroom instruction regarding level of learning objectives.

The student will ask questions about level of learning objectives.

Behavioral Verb Examples:

Ask	Follow
Choose	Give
Show interest	Uses
Identifies	Locates
Listens attentively	Select
Hold	Reply

Fig. 8.11 – Level of Learning Objective and Samples of Behavior for the Receiving Level

Level of Learning Objective and Samples of Behavior for the Responding Level

Level of Learning Objective:

The objective of this lesson is for each student to <u>respond</u> *positively to the importance of documenting level of learning objectives and samples of behavior.*

Samples of Behavior

The student will willingly answer questions regarding importance of documenting level of learning objectives and samples of behavior.

The student will help other students during classroom activities on the documentation of level of learning objectives and samples of behavior.

The student will conform to established rules when documenting level of learning objectives and samples of behavior.

Behavioral Verb Examples:

Answer	Comply
Obey	Perform
Assist	Help
Conform	Select
Report	Practice
Present	Practices

Fig. 8.12 – Level of Learning Objective and Samples of Behavior for the Responding Level

Level of Learning Objective and Samples of Behavior for the Valuing Level

Level of Learning Objective:

The objective of this lesson is for each student to value *the role of the strategy as an integral part of the lesson plan.*

Samples of Behavior

The student will initiate a discussion supporting the importance of clearly articulating the lesson strategy.

The student will actively participate in classroom discussion on developing a lesson strategy.

The student will voluntarily share examples of how developing strategies can benefit their own lesson plan development.

Behavioral Verb Examples:

Associate	Differentiate
Assume	Invite
Complete	Justify
Describe	Propose
Initiate	Join
Participate	Select
Work	Subscribe to
Share	Studies

Fig. 8.13 – Level of Learning Objective and Samples of Behavior for the Valuing Level

Level of Learning Objective and Samples of Behavior for the Organization Level

Level of Learning Objective:

The objective of this lesson is for each student to <u>organize</u> the *use of level-or-learning objectives into their own instructional design process.*

Samples of Behavior

Upon returning to their workplace, the student will integrate concept of level of learning objectives into their instructional design process.

The student will defend the value of level of learning objectives.

The student will articulate why they should integrate level of learning objectives into their instructional design process.

Behavioral Verb Examples:

Adhere to	Alter
Combine	Defend
Form judgments	Identify with
Integrate	Organize
Articulate	Plan
Arrange	Establish
Classify	Weigh alternatives

Fig. 8.14 – Level of Learning Objective and Samples of Behavior for the Organization Level

Level of Learning Objective and Samples of Behavior for the Characterization Level

Level of Learning Objective:

The objective of this lesson is for each student to <u>characterize</u> *structured instructional design.*

Samples of Behavior

Upon returning to their workplace, the student will propose the use of level of learning objectives.

The student will influence other training professionals to use of level of learning objectives.

The student will develop a philosophy that incorporates level of learning objectives.

Behavioral Verb Examples:

Develop philosophy	Judge issues
Influence	Propose
Act	Qualify
Change behavior	Serve
Question	Listen

Fig. 8.15 – Level of Learning Objective and Samples of Behavior for the Characterization Level

Part IV

TEACHING METHODS

After deciding the desired outcomes for a lesson, the instructor must determine how to teach it or what instructional method to use. Certain limiting factors may prevent an instructor from using certain instructional activities. In addition to considering the lesson objective, the instructor must consider the background and abilities of the learners, their motivation and learning styles, the number of learners, available facilities, the time, equipment, and money allotted to the lesson.

The selection of an instructional method may be a compromise between the method that is most suitable to the outcome (an ideal approach) and the method that is possible under the circumstances (a realistic approach). Many variations, combinations, and adaptations can be made of any method or methods of teaching; in fact, the number of possibilities is limited only by the instructor's imagination.

The first step in determining the most appropriate teaching method is to determine the domains of learning involved: cognitive and/or affective. Next, the instructor must deal with the realities of their situation—resources, space, class size, etc. In the subsequent chapters you will these items grouped as factors and constraints. Instructor expertise is always a consideration, particularly when the instruction contains complex procedures or involves the higher levels of cognitive and/or affective learning. Class size is a consideration. As student participation increases, it impacts the number of students each instructor can effectively manage. Evaluation becomes more difficult at the higher levels of learning some instructional methods provide ways for instructors to evaluate during the learning process. Case studies and other simulations are good examples because they require high levels of student activity that in turn provides opportunity to observe the students' behavior. The final criteria in determining the best teaching method is the degree that the method is responsive to individual student needs. Some instructional methods permit instructors to respond to individual student needs better than others. The lecture, for example, rates low in providing opportunities for instructors to modify their instruction in order to help the fast or slow learner. Small group methods, on the other hand, lend themselves to more individualized student treatment.

Other factors and constraints may also affect the selection of instructional methods. These additional considerations may be as significant as those discussed above and often combine to create even more difficult decisions regarding the selection of appropriate instructional methods. Among these other factors which affect the selection of instructional methods are the: need for a specially equipped facility, amount of time needed to develop instruction, cost to develop and maintain the hardware and software needed to support the method, and availability of support people to develop and maintain the hardware and software necessary to use the method effectively.

The quality of materials and adequate teaching skills must be available. Poorly prepared materials and weak instructor skills have a serious negative effect on all recommendations. Conversely, the "great teacher," the "master" of a particular instructional method, or extremely well prepared instructional materials may create an impact well beyond those normally expected.

Each of the following chapters will follow the same basic format in presenting an analysis of the various instructional methods. The methods are analyzed in their "pure" form, that is, not combined with other methods. Shown below is the format of the subsequent chapters, along with some definitions to help you better understand each instructional method and when it should be used to optimize the outcomes.

DEFINITION OF TERMS

Cognitive Domain—Lower Levels

Knowledge

The recall of previously learned material (facts or theories) in essentially the same form taught.

Comprehension

Seeing relationships, concepts, principles, and abstractions beyond simply remembering material. Typically involves translating, interpreting, and estimating future trends.

Cognitive Domain—Higher Levels

Application

The ability to use learned material in new and concrete situations, including the application of rules, methods, concepts, principles, laws, and theories.

Analysis

The ability to break down material into its component parts so that the organizational structure is understood, including the identification of the parts, analysis of the relationships between parts, and recognition of the organizational principles involved.

Synthesis

The ability to put parts together, forming new patterns or structures, such as a unique communication (a theme or speech), a plan of operations (a research proposal), or a set of abstract relations (schemes for classifying information.)

Evaluation

The ability to judge the value of material for a given purpose. Learning in this area is the highest in the cognitive hierarchy because it involves elements of all the other categories, plus conscious value judgments based on clearly defined criteria.

Affective Domain—Lower Levels

Receiving

The getting, holding, and directing of the student's attention, from the simple awareness that a thing exists to selective attention on the part of the learner.

Responding

The student not only attends to a particular phenomenon but also reacts to it in some way, such as acquiescence (reads assigned material), willingness to respond (voluntarily reads beyond assignment), or satisfaction in responding (reads for pleasure or enjoyment). Includes instructional objectives related to "interests" or "disinterests."

Affective Domain—Higher Levels

Valuing

The worth or value a student attaches to a particular object, phenomenon, or behavior, ranging from acceptance of a value to commitment. Includes instructional objectives related to "attitudes" and "appreciation."

Organization

The bringing together of different values, resolving conflicts among them, and building an internally consistent value system. Includes instructional objectives related to an integrated, coherent "philosophy of life."

Characterization

Pervasive, consistent, and predictable behavior (life style) developing from a value system that controls behavior for a significant period of time. Instructional objectives focusing on personal, social, and emotional adjustment are in this category.

Factors and Constraints.

Minimum level of instructor expertise

The minimum level of proficiency in the cognitive domain required to teach a particular method of instruction effectively. Unless an instructor is just delivering a lesson planned by an expert designer, most methods require the instructor to be at the application level or higher. In several instances throughout this chapter, the "one level higher rule" is recommended. Roughly translated, this rule cautions that instructors should be at least one cognitive level higher than the level of learning of the lesson being taught. If knowledge-level material is being taught, instructors should be at least at the comprehension level (or higher). If application level objectives are being used for a lesson, instructors should be at least at the analysis level of learning (or higher). In the affective domain, instructor expertise, which leads to instructor credibility, is essential to affecting student attitudes and belief systems.

Class size

The optimum number of students for teaching a particular method instruction. Recommended numbers (where applicable) are given in the narrative for each method. With ever ever-changing technology being integrated into today's classrooms, class size is extremely difficult to estimate.

Evaluation inherent in method

Does the method itself provide the basis for evaluating attainment of objectives, or is a follow-up evaluation device required?

Responsiveness to individual needs

Does the method allow for active student participation and produce opportunities to express viewpoints? Does the method allow for different levels of student achievement or allow students to work at their own pace?

CHAPTER 9

Lecture

The formal lecture is usually given to large groups (can be more than 100 people) with no active participation by the student. It is instructor-centered with virtually no interaction by the students. The learning experience is essentially passive.

COGNITIVE DOMAIN—LOWER LEVELS

Knowledge

Highly recommended when the basic purpose is to disseminate information and the material is not available elsewhere. It works well for arousing interest in a subject and in organizing content for presentation in a particular way for a specific group. It is especially suitable for content that must be continually updated or revised by the expert. However, the instructor should realize that material presented will be remembered for only a short time, unless it is reinforced through use of another teaching method or real-life experience.

Comprehension

Probably the most efficient at the knowledge level, but it may also be used at the comprehension level, particularly when the lecture is informal. Recommended if the student-instructor ratio is too high for small group activities. A more formal approach is recommended for a very specialized subject area if instructor expertise is at too low a level to use small group activities effectively.

COGNITIVE DOMAIN—HIGHER LEVELS

Many learners can increase their level of cognitive learning even at the higher levels. Learner motivation, need, and prerequisite skills are factors that must be considered. For all practical purposes, the expertise of the instructor must be at least one level higher than the educational outcome of the period.

AFFECTIVE DOMAIN—LOWER LEVELS

Not recommended.

AFFECTIVE DOMAIN—HIGHER LEVELS

Not recommended.

FACTORS AND CONSTRAINTS.

Minimum Level of Instructor Expertise

The at least one-level higher rule applies. For example, if a lecture is to the knowledge level, instructor expertise at the comprehension level is the minimum requirement.

Class Size

As long as the instructor can be seen and heard, the size of the class is not important. Under certain circumstances, an informal lecture to a small group may be just as defensible as a formal lecture to a larger one. In a very large hall, if students cannot be close enough to make eye contact with the lecturer, communication may suffer.

Evaluation Inherent in Method

Very little opportunity to estimate how well the students are learning the material exists, except in an informal lecture to a group of reasonable size.

Responsive to Individual Needs

Except in an informal lecture to a small group, lecturing usually does not allow students to formulate questions and have the questions answered before proceeding to the next area of instruction.

CHAPTER 10

Indirect Discourse

Indirect discourse is an interaction between two or more persons, one of whom may be the instructor, generally to present sharply opposing points of view for students. The dialogue is often highly structured towards preplanned goals and may take the form of questions and answers between the participants. Some examples of indirect discourse are panel discussions, teaching interviews, and dramatizations.

COGNITIVE DOMAIN—LOWER LEVELS

Knowledge

While these methods are cautiously recommended to teach factual information, many other methods are probably better suited at this cognitive level.

Comprehension

Especially suited for providing the bases for abstractions, for airing multiple points of view, and for drawing together data to form generalizations for the student to arrive at conclusions. These methods are suited to the development of student comprehension.

COGNITIVE DOMAIN—HIGHER LEVELS

Since there is little requirement for the students to put any abstractions to use in new situations, these methods are not generally recommended for the higher cognitive levels. These methods may provide an excellent basis for use at the higher levels particularly in combination with other methods.

AFFECTIVE DOMAIN—LOWER LEVELS

One great strength of indirect discourse is the development of lower level affective outcomes. These methods can go a long way toward encouraging student reception and response.

AFFECTIVE DOMAIN—HIGHER LEVELS

While it is possible to obtain valuing under certain circumstances, the higher affective levels are often beyond the scope of indirect discourse because, with the exception of question-and-answer periods, active student involvement and application are usually not possible. While indirect discourse may not generally be the first choice, it may prove to be effective at the higher affective levels in just the "right" situation.

FACTORS AND CONSTRAINTS

Minimum Level of Instructor Expertise

The methods of indirect discourse can best be used to develop knowledge and comprehension-level understanding. Often, however, they are suited to the higher levels of learning as long as the minimum level of instructor expertise follows the one-level higher rule.

Class Size

While there is no optimum class size for these methods, an advantage of indirect discourse is that it can be used for extremely large groups of students, as long as they can see and hear.

Evaluation Inherent in Method

The measurement or evaluation of student learning is not an inherent part of indirect discourse. The instructor has no way of knowing at the end of the lesson whether the students have learned. Some additional form of evaluation is necessary to determine that students have met the planned objectives. The only exception would be a question-and-answer period where the nature and quality of student questions might be an indirect way of evaluating students. Not all students, however, may get to ask questions and others may choose not to ask them.

Responsive to Individual Needs

If these methods do not include a question-and-answer period, as is often the case, they are not very responsive to individual needs. Issues or questions of interest will never surface unless students are allowed to pursue them in some way. By themselves, the methods of indirect discourse do not permit students' needs to be satisfied.

CHAPTER 11

Reading

Reading is when students are given reading assignments as the main learning activity. Overall effectiveness is greatly increased when it is followed up with another more interactive method.

COGNITIVE DOMAIN—LOWER LEVELS

Knowledge

For the majority of students, the most effective and time-efficient means of presenting knowledge-level material. They can proceed at their own pace and are free to adjust to the learning experience. They are limited only by reading speed and comprehension, both of which may be improved through special courses.

Comprehension

Although a student can reach the comprehension level through carefully selected readings, other methods that ensure interaction with the instructor or other students are preferable. When such interaction is not possible, reading assignments may be an acceptable alternative, especially when combined with study or review questions or other activities that require the student to manipulate the material.

COGNITIVE DOMAIN—HIGHER LEVELS

Caution must be used at the higher cognitive levels of developmental learning. While, it is possible that a learner can be taken through one or more of the higher levels with an in-depth, lengthy, carefully planned reading program, it is not recommended.

AFFECTIVE DOMAIN—LOWER LEVELS

Whether attitudes can be influenced through reading depends on such factors as the writer's skills and the learner's predisposition. Therefore, reading is recommended for teaching the lower level of the affective domain (receiving and responding) only. There can be no assurance that any of the higher levels will be reached.

AFFECTIVE DOMAIN—HIGHER LEVELS

Because of individual differences, it is difficult to be sure that reading materials will actually lead to the desired higher-level affective objectives. But, we all can identify with the learner who is deeply moved or profoundly affected by a written work. Reading, by itself, will not provide evidence of change at the higher affective levels. It may, however, be the vehicle for significant progression up the affective developmental ladder when combined with other methods. Learners at the very highest affective levels will plan their own reading programs for learning.

FACTORS AND CONSTRAINTS

Minimum Level of Instructor Expertise

Because the instructor's only control in this method is the selection of what students read or the direction of their research, the instructor's expertise should be at the higher levels of the cognitive taxonomy.

Class Size

Class size is a factor in reading only when all members of a class must have access to a limited number of copies of a particular reading. With preplanning and/or duplication, such problems are easy to avoid. Some techniques for making reading materials more available to students are textbook issue (especially a "walking library"), reserve book rooms or shelves, classroom bookshelves, electronic versions, and multiple library copies. For an effective research program specialized facilities such as libraries, archives, reference materials, and staff are essential.

Evaluation Inherent in Method

Evaluation is not built into the method so the instructor must provide evaluation separately.

Responsive to Individual Needs

Although reading is highly responsive to the needs and differences of individual students, the instructor must not neglect the factor of student motivation. Many students do not like to read or have not developed disciplined study habits. Also, some students may have low reading speed and/or problems with reading comprehension. Because the instructor is normally not present when the reading takes place, controls and well-defined goals are all the more important.

CHAPTER 12

Self-Paced Methods

Self-paces methods are programmed instruction such as video or computer-based learning. Since this method usually stands alone and is not normally followed up with an interactive method, there is little chance of recovering lost opportunities for learning.

COGNITIVE DOMAIN—ALL LEVELS

The wide-ranging applications of the various self-paced methodologies indicate potential for all of the cognitive levels. Great numbers of learners have mastered basic factual information as well as advanced concepts and principles through the use of programmed instruction and mediated objectives from simple knowledge to complex tasks requiring application level and beyond. Materials and methods such as these are very tolerant of learners, permitting them to select their own pace of learning, review the material as they see fit, and redo the lesson until the material has been mastered. These characteristics allow self-paced methods to accommodate individual learning rates, styles, and methods for cognitive objectives.

AFFECTIVE DOMAIN—LOWER LEVELS

Most of the methods that have man-material or man-machine inter-action rather than human interaction may be cautiously recommended for affective development. Self-paced methods may enhance a student's attitude towards the subject matter, but they are unlikely to effect change in value systems or to help reach higher affective levels.

AFFECTIVE DOMAIN—HIGHER LEVELS

On the other hand, it is possible to construct a self-paced methodology that will enhance a learner's abilities to progress through the levels of the affective taxonomy. As more and more progress is made in the use of computer-based learning, it is likely that the higher levels of the affective taxonomy will be affected by such tools.

FACTORS AND CONSTRAINTS

Minimum Level of Instructor Expertise

Preparing materials for use in the self-paced methods requires a very high level of instructor expertise in the subject matter, perhaps rivaled only by simulation and case study methodology. Self-paced methods also require considerable technical skill in their design. Programmed instruction and modules demand careful attention to a fairly rigid set of rules as well as considerable development time and field-testing. This requirement for both subject matter and technical expertise puts the various self-paced methods among the most difficult, time-consuming, and costly to produce. The benefits realized from the methods must be carefully weighed against these factors.

Class Size

By the nature of their construction, self-paced exercises are directed towards individualized learning. Because most of these exercises are capable of being mass-produced, large audiences can be reached by these methods, although the mode of delivery is individualized.

Evaluation Inherent in Method

A basic ingredient in all self-paced instruction is ongoing evaluation of learner progress towards established learning objectives. Many forms of self-paced instruction have carefully prepared systems for pre-, post-, and formative testing. Often the evaluation step is so intermingled in the instructional materials that the learner may not consider it to be a "test" in the usual sense.

Responsive to Individual Needs

Particularly responsive to student needs and differences. Properly prepared, the methods can incorporate such sound learning principles as positive reinforcement and immediate feedback. These principles allow students with various needs and motivation levels to be successful. In addition, various technical treatment such as branching programs (special tracks) provide additional capacity to deal with individual needs and differences.

CHAPTER 13

Questioning

Questioning as a tool is used to emphasize a point, stimulate thinking, keep students alert, check understanding, review material, and seek clarification. While sometimes referred to as the Socratic method; instruction by asking students questions is a method as old as ancient Greece and as modern as a law schools. Questioning as a method may resemble a guided discussion, but the goal is often to obtain specific answers to specific questions (reiteration) and not to stimulate discussion. An instructor may use the method for "trapping" students into inconsistencies in logic, which will sharpen their thinking skills. Law professors often use the method for "interrogating" specific students using a series of questions as they might be used in a court of law.

COGNITIVE DOMAIN—LOWER LEVELS

Knowledge

Although possible at the knowledge level, not generally recommended because most questioning results in too much recitation and response in an elementary, rote-learning classroom manner. Other methods may be more productively used for the presentation and reinforcement of knowledge-level material.

Comprehension

Lends itself best to material at this level because the instructor can lead the student or class to form concepts, test them, and see their inter-relationships through a series of skillfully chosen questions.

COGNITIVE DOMAIN—HIGHER LEVELS

All Levels

Although it is possible to question at the higher cognitive levels (application, analysis, synthesis, and evaluation), these levels lend themselves to more student interaction than is common with one-on-one questioning. Questioning can be used to stimulate thinking at the higher levels as a preliminary step for the student.

FACTORS AND CONSTRAINTS

Minimum Level of Instructor Expertise

For fully exploiting the potential of the questioning method, instructors should be at the evaluation level, that is, highly skilled, because the method requires immediate evaluation of student responses and expert competence in the subject to see the logical consequences of a line of reasoning or to form new problem solving approaches. Instructors with an especially analytical mind who enjoy the give and take of lively interchange will find this method effective in achieving instructional objectives.

Class Size

Although reportedly some business and law schools use the questioning method to good purpose in very large lecture halls (100 and more students), the method lends itself best to one-on-one or small group (8-12) instruction.

Evaluation Inherent in Method

The fact that instructors receive immediate response to their questions and are in a position to evaluate these responses before proceeding to the next question rates this aspect very high.

Responsive to Individual Needs

If the instructor is able to use a number of spontaneous questions instead of relying on planned questions, the method can be very responsive to student needs and differences.

CHAPTER 14

Non-Directed Discussion

Non-directed discussion is a group interactive process in which task or objective-related information and experiences are evoked from the student. The instructor normally plays a very limited or passive role. The peer-controlled seminar is a group of peers who meet for the exchange of ideas, usually in the form of prepared papers with discussion or questions following. When used, the instructor should provide a statement of the educational objectives, a suggested discussion guide, and should require some tangible evidence of the results of the discussion.

COGNITIVE DOMAIN—ALL LEVELS

Although the peer-controlled seminar can successfully discuss both lower and higher level cognitive materials, there is the danger that the seminar will pool ignorance. Clearly defined objectives and a means of measuring their achievement can, however, provide the focus for learning at any cognitive level. Such learning can be substantial.

AFFECTIVE DOMAIN—LOWER LEVELS

A basic use for the peer-controlled seminar is receiving and responding to affective material. A possible use in corporate training might be for seminar discussion following a guest speaker (such as a subject matter expert on a relevant subject) whose primary reason for addressing the group was motivational. If properly motivated, the group might share and reinforce the affective experience among themselves, but without strong motivation and interest event this limited objective might not be met and the session might just as easily deteriorate into free discussion.

AFFECTIVE DOMAIN—HIGHER LEVELS

Under the proper conditions non-directed discussion can be used to further affective learning at the higher levels. Motivated learners pursuing a common goal can share a powerful learning experience with or without an instructor being present to direct the flow of an unstructured discussion. The obvious caution still exists as with the lower affective level, but student-controlled discussion can be and is a powerful tool for affective development.

FACTORS AND CONSTRAINTS

Minimum Level of Instructor Expertise

Not applicable, because of the instructor's limited or passive role in a peer-controlled seminar that, is also one of its weaknesses. If qualified students are available and properly supervised, such seminars can still be highly successful.

Class Size

The small group (8-12 students) is probably the most common and workable size for the peer-controlled seminar. Larger classes will be too unwieldy.

Evaluation Inherent in Method

With the instructor playing a passive role there is little evaluation in the usual sense. However, it is possible to obtain evaluation information if an individual or group product is required.

Responsive to Individual Needs

As the seminar is entirely run by the students, it is obviously responsive to individual interests, but not necessarily to their educational needs. There is the danger, however, that more vocal students in the group will dominate the class to the exclusion of quieter students to their detriment.

CHAPTER 15

Guided Discussion

The guided discussion is an instructor-controlled, interactive process of sharing information and experiences related to achieving an educational objective. The difference between non-directed discussion and guided discussion is the active involvement of the instructor in asking questions and summarizing the concepts and principles learned. The instructor interacts with the group as a whole through questions, but tries not to dominate the discussion. Students are encouraged to learn about a subject by actively sharing ideas, knowledge, and opinions. The flow of communication is a transaction among all the students rather than question and response between individual students and the instructor.

COGNITIVE DOMAIN—LOWER LEVELS

Knowledge

Not particularly recommended for simple recall of factual information. Other methods such as the lecture, reading, or self-directed instruction are more efficient for reaching this level. On the other hand, for many learners, such results can be enhanced by participating in guided discussions because they can interact with the content rather than passively taking lecture notes.

Comprehension

Designed primarily for this level and is one of the most efficient ways of reaching it. The method develops concepts and principles through group process and the unobtrusive guidance of the instructor. Properly conducted, the guided discussion also ensures that each student learns at this level, as the instructor can draw out an individual student who may not be participating voluntarily. Unlike free discussion, which probably has no objective and which develops solely by the natural direction the group happens to take, the guided discussion is highly structured, with planned questions that lead the group to a specific, predetermined learning objective.

COGNITIVE DOMAIN—HIGHER LEVELS

Rarely reaches the higher levels of learning as students are not required to put the concepts they have learned to use in new situations as in some of the application methods. It is not unusual for a group to pursue problem solving (and it's component skills of analysis, synthesis, and evaluation) during a discussion that is "guided." The goals of the group, their motivation, their prerequisite skills, etc., must be taken into account when looking to the guided discussion as a tool for developing the higher cognitive levels.

AFFECTIVE DOMAIN—ALL LEVELS

By participating in a guided discussion, students are exposed to the opinions of others and may be forced to defend their personal positions. For this reason, the method is more generally suited to receiving, responding and valuing than to organization and characterization. The method can and often does work at the higher levels as well, however, and should be considered when lesson planning for higher affective outcomes.

FACTORS AND CONSTRAINTS

Minimum Level of Instructor Expertise

Although it is possible for instructors in guided discussions to be at the comprehension level, ideally they should be at the higher cognitive levels. One primary responsibility of instructors is the ability to judge the worth of student responses, since achieving the planned objective is totally dependent on the use of student responses to form the generalization. Since instructors cannot possibly use all student responses, they must have the ability to select those that are most relevant to the concept or principle under discussion. As the method is a new one for most instructors, a certain amount of training is necessary, but once an instructor has the basic idea, there is no difficulty in applying the technique to different situations.

Certain skills, distinct from expertise in the subject being taught, are needed to conduct a successful guided discussion. The instructor should control the group so that discussion flows among the students. Leadoff and follow-up questions are asked as they were planned, but spontaneous questions should also be used frequently to clarify student responses and eliminate errors in fact and reasoning. The instructor should avoid biasing the discussion or withholding necessary information from the students. All students should be encouraged to participate, and positive reinforcement should be given to student inputs.

Class Size

Although 8-12 students might be considered an optimum size, the method can be used very satisfactorily with a slightly larger or smaller group. However, as the size of the group moves above the optimum, it becomes somewhat harder to control the discussion, thus calling for more instructor expertise in conducting discussions.

Evaluation Inherent in Method

Since students are not normally asked to actually formulate and verbally express their own generalizations, some other type of follow-on evaluation device is necessary. However, if time is available and if students can be asked to express their own generalizations, then instructors might be able to evaluate achievement of the objective.

Responsive to Individual Needs

Does an excellent job of meeting individual needs. Each student is encouraged to express opinions on issues and to ask questions about issues raised by others. The guided discussion is organized to encourage maximum student participation. In the overview the instructor tells students what will be discussed, gives any necessary definitions or concepts, and encourages participation. Carefully planned leadoff and follow-up questions then elicit this participation. The instructor should also anticipate possible student responses and include these in the teaching plan. Although remotivation and closure are planned, the final summary can developed using inputs from the students.

CHAPTER 16

Individual Project

Students are assigned specific projects to be completed either during, or within a specified period of time following, the course. The completion of the assigned project will require the student to progress through the taxonomy of learning until they reach the level for which the objective calls for. If possible, the project should be directly related to a requirement of the student's job and thereby includes a certain degree of motivation.

COGNITIVE DOMAIN—LOWER LEVELS

Can be used to teach at these levels, but they do not require the method's full potential. Usually students will need to acquire mastery at these levels before the project starts through other means such as reading.

COGNITIVE DOMAIN—HIGHER LEVELS

One of the best methods for ensuring learning at the higher levels of application, analysis, synthesis, and evaluation—all of which are difficult to reach by most other means. Properly directed, individual research gives the students maximum flexibility to pursue interests at their own speed, while at the same time allowing them to reach their capabilities and maximum insights. Individual projects allow the student to work independently and also interact with peers and the instructor.

AFFECTIVE DOMAIN—LOWER LEVELS

Students could be influenced affectively during an individual project to pay attention (receive) and actually take some action (respond) to the material. However, for the most part, receiving and responding skills are assumed to be already present before a student undertakes a project.

AFFECTIVE DOMAIN—HIGHER LEVELS

An excellent means by which attainment of the higher affective levels may be judged. Whether a student values certain materials, techniques, or ideas is often easy to determine during the conduct of a project. The same can be said of organization and characterization as well. Frequent contacts between student and instructor are an important part of the method. They provide the opportunity for regular feedback and guidance. The instructor who is properly attuned to what to look for will find indicators of the higher affective levels in this method.

FACTORS AND CONSTRAINTS

Minimum Level of Instructor Expertise

Since the higher cognitive levels are desired in this method and since students will be required to sift through and evaluate data, equipment, or persons, it is essential that the instructor be operating at the higher levels of the cognitive taxonomy.

Class Size

The actual instruction and interaction between student and instructor is usually on a one-to-one basis. There is a practical limit to the number of individual projects that can be supervised at one time. An outstanding but time consuming method.

Evaluation Inherent in Method

Because student and instructor interact regularly and because finished portions of the project are evaluated and feedback is given as the endeavor proceeds, it is clear that student progress is monitored constantly. Obviously, knowledge of what students must be able to do and how they are doing it is readily available.

Responsive to Individual Needs

With the continual interchange between instructor and student, instructors will find it easy to identify and deal with students' special weaknesses, interests, and needs.

CHAPTER 17

Field Trip

A field trip is an out of class learning activity. Students take a trip away from the classroom to a particular place relevant to the objectives of the course or class. Students are told beforehand, or at the time of the visit, about certain things to observe.

COGNITIVE DOMAIN—ALL LEVELS

With some exceptions, field trips are typically used for affective purposes rather than for measurable cognitive development. For this reason, it may be difficult to visualize how comprehension, application, and the higher levels can be developed in the student as the result of a field trip. Certainly some cognition may be developed—in some cases a great deal of cognition—but one would not highly recommend the field trip for this purpose since there may be other more appropriate methods (for example, lecture, reading, etc.) available.

AFFECTIVE DOMAIN—ALL LEVELS

Highly recommended as a method to influence all levels of student affect. The field trip experience may gain the attention of some students (receiving) and evoke responses in others (responding). Value or worth may be seen in an object or idea as the result of a field trip and, while it is difficult to attain, this method can be a strong factor in the achievement of even the highest affective levels.

FACTORS AND CONSTRAINTS

Minimum Level of Instructor Expertise

An instructor need not be at the highest cognitive levels to participate in a useful field trip for students. However, the instructor must be at the comprehension level at least in order to make proper use of the method. The selection of the field trip location and activities, the asking of meaningful questions during the trip, and the possible discussion of the trip afterward would all require comprehension on the part of the instructor. Since the field trip may be used primarily for affective purposes, it is recommended that the instructor be at the higher levels of affective taxonomy as well.

Class Size

Many variables determine optimum class size for a field trip, but the number of students per instructor should be small. All students need to observe and experience the important elements of the field trip and be able to interact with either the instructor or an expert at the field trip site.

Evaluation Inherent in Method

As an experiential teaching method, formal evaluation is generally not possible. Some additional form of evaluation would be necessary to measure achievement of the instructional objective.

Responsive to Individual Needs

Generally speaking field trips are not a method that meets an individual student's needs. The typical field trip is a highly structured and scheduled affair that leaves little time for students to satisfy their needs with regard to the topic. The addition of a question-and-answer period helps in this regard, as do post-field trip discussions.

CHAPTER 18

Simulation

There are a number of completely different approaches to simulation, although the theory is the same—a real life situation is simulated and the students have to perform their roles. For instance, an airline pilot will learn to perform certain roles in a flight simulator, in which every possible element of certain flight situations are prepared and then the pilot is then required to perform the role in its artificial surrounds. In this way the pilot can be prepared for all types of emergencies without risking an airplane! But it is possible to simulate actual work situations. For instance, at a workshop on panel interviews, the instructor prepared a full panel and participants in the workshop were required to perform the roles of a situation when panel members disagreed about whether a person should be hired or not.

Preparing a simulation is a time consuming process but one in which students can learn a great deal about actual situations, so that they can prepare themselves in advance for situations which they might find themselves in at a later time.

COGNITIVE DOMAIN—LOWER LEVELS

Knowledge

Not usually recommended for imparting knowledge to students. As a matter of fact, knowledge is presumed to be a prerequisite for this method in most cases.

Comprehension

While simulation can be a vehicle through which the development of comprehension can occur, most simulations assume a prerequisite of comprehension level functioning.

COGNITIVE DOMAIN—HIGHER LEVELS

One strength is the provision of an opportunity for students to operate at the highest cognitive levels within a low risk environment. Most simulations require some sort of analysis, synthesis, and evaluation, while practically all simulations require the application of concepts and principles in new situations.

AFFECTIVE DOMAIN—ALL LEVELS

Another strength is the direct relevance to affective development. Simulation can be instrumental in the achievement of all affective levels. For example, observing or participating in a simulation may be responsible for student attention and action (receiving and responding). Since the simulation deals with putting learned material to use, the higher affective levels are also addressed. Students begin to see worth or value in certain principles, ideas, equipment, etc., and this insight is the stepping-stone to the higher affective levels.

FACTORS AND CONSTRAINTS

Minimum Level of Instructor Expertise

The instructor must be at the highest cognitive level possible to use simulations effectively. Since the students are often operating at the highest levels, it is essential that the instructor also be with them at these levels. Though more passive in this method than in some others, the instructor must be ready to act and answer upon request or whenever the situation dictates.

Class Size

While there may be large numbers of students involved in any given simulation, there must be few students per instructor during the simulation itself. Without this guidance, students will flounder and not get out of the simulation what they might and should get.

Evaluation Inherent in Method

Most simulations provide immediate feedback to instructor and student alike. Unless one is interested in measuring knowledge or comprehension prerequisites or post-simulation outcomes, the proof of learning in a simulation is the adequate handling of whatever task is involved, and often no other evaluative device is required.

Responsive to Individual Needs

Because of the simulator-student and instructor-student interaction and immediate feedback, simulations do provide for individual student needs. Various simulations or portions of simulations can be run and repeated until adequately dealt with by the student (achievement of instructional objectives). Weaknesses and strengths can be quickly identified and worked with as appropriate.

CHAPTER 19

Case Study

Many corporate trainers teach abstract or mental skills, the theory of a job—like strategies for managing meetings—or an aspect of leadership. In courses where the subjects are abstract, however, students tend to be less involved with the specific tasks they will encounter later, on the job. Theory and practice may be far apart. The case study is generally an excellent method for use in the type of corporate training.

Despite the obvious strengths of the case method as a teaching tool in the business environment, it is not being utilized to its fullest potential. In an effort to increase both the understanding and use of this highly effective teaching method, a detailed discussion on the use of the case study is included at appendix A. This is an extremely powerful method for taking students to the higher levels of both the cognitive and affective domains.

COGNITIVE DOMAIN—LOWER LEVELS

Knowledge

Not usually recommended for imparting knowledge to students. As a matter of fact, knowledge is presumed to be a prerequisite for this method in most cases.

Comprehension

While simulation can be a vehicle through which the development of comprehension can occur, most cases assume a prerequisite of comprehension level functioning. Although the case study can be used to teach to this level, normally other methods such as the guided discussion or the controlled conversation methods are more efficient.

COGNITIVE DOMAIN—HIGHER LEVELS

One of the best teaching methods for reaching the higher levels of the cognitive domain. Very effective both for applying a single principle or concept and for evaluating a situation involving total analysis and synthesis. The primary limitation is the absolute necessity for students to have a thorough comprehension of the concepts and principles involved before the case study begins. For this reason, the method is often used as a "capstone" to other methods at the end of a block of instruction.

AFFECTIVE DOMAIN—LOWER LEVELS

The use of the case study in this domain very closely parallels its use in the cognitive domain. Although a good method for reaching lower level objectives, other methods such as the guided discussion and field trips may be more efficient if the affective objectives are solely at the lower levels.

AFFECTIVE DOMAIN—HIGHER LEVELS

Highly recommended for the higher levels as students are forced to recognize the role of systematic planning and objective approaches to problem solving. They are also forced to defend positions that in many cases are a synthesis of their own value systems.

FACTORS AND CONSTRAINTS

Minimum Level of Instructor Expertise

The instructor must be at the highest cognitive level possible to use cases effectively. Since the students are often operating at the highest levels, it is essential that the instructor also be with them at these levels. Though more passive in this method than in some others, the instructor must be ready to act and answer upon request or whenever the situation dictates.

Class Size

Class size in the case study method is perhaps more a function of time than any other one factor. All students must be prepared to present their thoughts on the subject under consideration. Time must be available for other students or the instructor to critically analyze the proposals presented by each student. Although some authors writing on the case study recommended 8-12 students as an optimum number, a variation is used quite satisfactorily in large classes where adequate time and facilities are available.

Evaluation Inherent in Method

Since students must give their own proposals or at least critically analyze the proposals of others, the instructor has an excellent opportunity for on-the-spot evaluation of student achievement of objectives. Under optimum conditions, no follow-up evaluation may be necessary.

In a great number of instances, written or selection tests are successfully used to measure achievement of learning outcomes.

Responsive to Individual Needs

Since students are free to develop their own approaches to the situation, the method is easily accommodated to individual student needs, differences, and creativity.

Part V

ORGANIZATIONAL PATTERNS

After we have selected the appropriate instructional method we must decide how to organize the lesson. Every lesson needs an introduction, body, and conclusion. In most instances the body of the lesson should be prepared before the introduction or conclusion. After we prepare the body or main part of the lesson, we will be in a better position to begin or conclude the lesson. The first consideration in planning the body is how to organize the main points, but organization of sub-points is also important. Well thought out sequencing of the main points and sub-points of a lesson will help both the instructor and the students—the instructor in teaching and the students in learning. Most lessons, regardless of their length, divide nicely into from two to five main points.

The typical ways of organizing main or sub-points of a lesson are by the patterns of time, space, cause-effect, problem-solution, pro-con, or topic. Furthermore, certain strategies can be used with each pattern from known to unknown, for instance, or from simple to complex. How does an instructor decide which patterns and strategies to use? The lesson material will often organize itself more easily with one pattern and strategy than with another. Let us consider how various patterns and strategies can be used to organize the main points of a lesson.

CHAPTER 20

Time

Our vocabularies are filled with words which refer to time: now, tomorrow, yesterday, today, sooner, later, earlier, last week, a month from now, four years ago, next time. We work, play, sleep, and eat at certain times. Major events in our lives are organized by time: births, engagements, marriages, deaths, etc. Time or the chronological pattern of lesson organization is a natural way of arranging events in the sequence of order in which they happened, or in giving directions in the order to be followed in carrying them out. This kind of organization is sometimes called sequential organization. Certain processes, procedures, or historical movements and developments can often be explained best with a time sequence pattern.

Example of a Time-based Organizational Pattern

- The medical technician presenting a lesson on mouth-to-mouth resuscitation would probably use the time order for the main points: (1) preliminary steps—proper body position, mouth open, tongue and jaw forward, (2) the mouth-to-mouth process, (3) caring for the patient once breathing resumes.

Fig. 20.1 – Time-based Organization Pattern

Any lesson on a subject with several phases lends itself well to the time pattern. For example, given an objective for students to know the three planned phases of the European Union (where phase one was to precede phase two, and phase two precede phase three), a lesson might have these main points: (1) Phase one—a customs union where nations agreed to reduce duties, (2) Phase two—an economic union using a common currency and (3) Phase three—a political union with national representatives as members of a common parliament.

Of course, rather than looking forward in time from a given moment, the strategy might be to look backward from a point in time. In other words, the strategy might be to move from recent to earlier time rather than from early to late. Regardless of which strategy is used, the flow of the lesson and the transitions should make the chronological relationships between main points clear to the students.

CHAPTER 21

Space

A spatial or geographical pattern is effective in describing relationships. When using this pattern, the lesson material is developed according to some directional strategy such as east to west or north to south. For example, if an instructor were conducting orientation training for new employees, the lesson may be divided into sections on the various regions serviced by the organization.

With lessons about certain objects, the strategy might be to arrange the main points from top to bottom or bottom to top.

Example of a Space-based Organizational Pattern

- A new hire orientation would present the organizational chart from the highest ranks to the lowest in the organization.

Fig. 21.1 – Space-based Organization Pattern

In all lessons arranged spatially, we need to introduce each aspect or main point according to some strategy. Just as with a lesson organized by time, the subject matter and the transitions should include elaboration and clarification of how the main points relate to one another. A simple listing of the various objects or places without elaboration as to how they are related may confuse the students and make the points harder to remember.

CHAPTER 22

Cause/Effect

A cause/effect pattern of organization is used in a lesson where one set of conditions is given as a cause for another set. In such lessons we may use one of two basic strategies to arrange our main points. With a cause/effect strategy, we begin with a given set of conditions and show that these will produce or have already produced certain results or effects. With an effect-cause strategy, we take a certain set of conditions as the effects and allege that they resulted from certain causes.

Example of a Cause/Effect-based Organizational Pattern

- Cause-Effect: When presenting a lesson concerning women in leadership roles the lesson might first discuss the increasing number of women in the work force and then make the linkage to women assuming more responsible leadership roles.

- Effect-Cause: When presenting a lesson on child abuse the first point might explain the effects of child abuse upon the children themselves, the parents, and even on society. The second point might suggest that the causes are that parents themselves were abused as children or that they lack proper education on parenting.

Fig. 22.1 – Cause/Effect-based Organization Pattern

Whichever strategy is used, two cautions must be observed: (1) Beware of false causes. Just because one event or circumstance precedes another does not mean that the former causes the latter. Many persons assume that "First A happened, and then B took place, so A must have caused B." (2) Beware of single causes. Few things result from a single cause. There may be several causes and they may not act independently. Their effect may be greater or less than the sum of their parts. Lack of safety features on automobiles does not by itself cause most highway accidents, but this cause plus careless driving and unsafe highways may, in combination, account for many highway accidents.

CHAPTER 23

Problem/Solution

This pattern, sometimes called the disease-remedy pattern or the need-satisfaction pattern, presents students with a problem and then proposes a way to solve it. With this pattern we must show that a problem exists and then offer a corrective action that is (1) practical, (2) desirable, (3) capable of being put into action, and (4) able to relieve the problem. It must also be one that does not introduce new and worse evils of its own.

There are different strategies we might employ when using the problem/solution method. If the students are aware of the problem and the possible solutions, we might discuss the problem briefly, mention the possible solutions, and then spend more time in showing why one solution is better than others.

Example of a Problem/Solution-based Organizational Pattern

- When presenting a lesson where the objective is for each student to comprehend that solar energy is the best solution to the energy crisis. The main points might be (1) the world is caught in the grip of an energy crisis, (2) several solutions are possible, and (3) solar energy is the best long-term solution.

Fig. 23.1 – Problem/Solution-based Organization Pattern

If the students are not aware of the problem or need, we may describe in detail the exact nature of the problem. Sometimes when students become aware of the problem, the solution becomes evident, and little time is needed to develop the solution in the lesson. At other times we need to spend time developing both the problem and the solution.

Still another strategy is to alternate or stagger portions of the problem with portions of the solution. For example, the cost of a project may be seen as one problem, workability another, time to do the project as a third. Taking each in turn and providing solutions to cost, work ability, and time as we present these aspects of the problem may be more satisfying to students than if we had discussed all of the problem and then its total solution.

Whatever strategy is used, with the problem/solution pattern students must become aware that a problem exists before a solution will be agreed upon.

CHAPTER 24

Pro/Con

The pro/con pattern, sometimes called the for-against pattern or advantages-disadvantages pattern, is similar to a problem-solution pattern in that the lesson is usually planned so as to lead to a conclusion. A major difference, however, is that fairly even attention is usually directed toward both sides of an issue with a pro/con pattern.

Table ?.1 - Example of a Pro/Con-based Organizational Pattern
• When presenting a lesson on the effects of jogging on individual health. The first main point may be to list present the positive effects jogging can have on health and the second main point may be to present the factors that make jogging problematic.

Fig. 24.1 – Pro/Con-based Organization Pattern

There are various strategies to consider when using the pro/con pattern. One consideration is whether to present pro or con first. Another is whether to present both sides and let students draw their own conclusions or to present the material in such a way that students are led to accept the "school solution".

Then we must decide whether to let students decide for themselves whether the advantages outweigh the disadvantages. Pro/con plus one is the label given to the organization used when we draw a final conclusion based on the two sides.

When deciding the specific strategy to use with the pro/con pattern and determining how much time to spend on each, the following guidelines may be helpful: (1) giving both sides fairly even emphasis is most effective when the weight of evidence is clearly on the favored side; (2) presenting both sides is more effective when students may be initially opposed to the school solution; (3) presenting only the favored side is most effective when students already favor the school solution or conclusion; (4) presenting the favored side last is generally more favorable to its acceptance, especially if the side not favored is not shown in too strong a light.

CHAPTER 25

Topical

A topical division of the main points of a lesson involves determining categories of the subject or lesson objective. This type of categorizing or classifying often springs directly from the subject itself.

Example of a Topical Organizational Pattern

- When presenting a lesson to new students regarding courses at college. The population would be divided into topical divisions of freshmen, sophomores, juniors, and seniors, with each class division serving as a main point.

Fig. 25.1 – Topic-based Organization Pattern

At times the material itself suggests certain strategies for ordering the main points. For instance, a lesson on levels-of-learning would most likely begin with the knowledge-level as the first main point, since knowledge-level lessons are generally simpler to understand. Then the lesson would move on through the hierarchy to comprehension, application, analysis, synthesis, and finally evaluation levels. In other words, our lesson would follow a simple-to-complex strategy in organizing the "topics" or levels-of-learning.

Other topically organized lessons might follow strategies of known to unknown, general to specific, or specific to general. The number of strategies for arranging topical main points is practically infinite. The important consideration, as with any pattern, is that we give thought to the strategy of arrangement in order to improve student understanding and learning.

CHAPTER 26

Combining Organizational Patterns

If we use a single pattern to organize the main points, our lessons will make more sense. We will be able to remember more readily what the main points are when we teach the lesson. Even more important, students will be able to follow the lesson more easily and retain the material if we use a single, logical pattern of organization.

While we may choose a certain organizational pattern for the main points, we may decide to use different patterns for sub-points.

Example of Mixing Organizational Patterns
• When presenting a lesson with an objective for each student to know the importance of nonverbal factors of communication.
o The main points (I. Performance Factors and II. Nonperformance Factors) are arranged topically.
o The sub-points for main point I (upper, middle, and lower body) are organized spatially.
o A pro-con pattern is followed in discussing positive and negative effects from each body performance factor.
o The sub-points for main point II (objects, space, and time) are organized topically as are the two sub-points under space.

Fig. 26.1 – Mixing Organization Patterns

The important thing to remember is that each set of main points or sub-points should follow a given pattern of organization.

Of course, it may be that none of the formal patterns of organization discussed in this chapter adequately fits our content. If this is the case, we must simply strive to organize our lesson in the way that will help present the information to our students in the most meaningful fashion. As we construct our tentative outline, we must do so with our students' needs in mind. But whatever pattern or strategy we choose, it should be a conscious and rational choice and we should be able to defend or explain it.

Part VI

INSTRUCTOR'S GUIDE

So far in the instructional design process we have covered what we want the student to learn (level of learning objectives), how we will evaluate (samples of behavior), the method will use to present the material (teaching method), and the sequence we will present those materials (organizational pattern). It is now time to pull all these components together into a package called the Instructor's Guide. This guide includes two documents: the lesson plan and the teaching plan. All the instructional design information developed is documented in the lesson plan. The actual material to be presented is documented in the teaching plan. Both of these documents are covered in subsequent chapters and an example is included at appendix B.

Instructor Guides can be prepared several ways. In larger organizations with multiple instructors, it is common to develop a detailed lesson plan, and then have each instructor develop their own teaching plan. This way, each session is geared towards the same objectives and all instructors use the same overall strategy; while providing each instructor with the flexibility to design their own delivery around their own strengths and experiences. In other organizations, where greater control how the material is delivered is desired, both the lesson and teaching plans may be developed and each instructor is expected to deliver the material in the same way.

Another variation is the level of detail contained in the teaching plan. Some instructors use outline form to document the material they plan to deliver. Others actually write out the material in manuscript form as if the intent was to read it. Both ways are acceptable depending on the preferences of the instructor, but the latter runs the risk of turning into a crutch and being read like a script. On the other hand, used correctly, the manuscript method provides a valuable resource in practicing delivery or in transferring the knowledge to another instructor.

CHAPTER 27

Lesson Plan

Listed below is an item by item breakout for each part of the lesson plan, If the item is covered in previous chapters, you will be referred to that chapter, otherwise, it will be discussed in this chapter. The purpose of this section is to serve as a quick reference for each part.

DEVELOPED BY

This is simply a means to demonstrate who developed the lesson plan.

COURSE LENGTH

This states the course duration.

LESSON OBJECTIVES

Covered in chapter 8.

SAMPLES OF BEHAVIOR

Covered in chapter 8.

TEACHING METHOD

Covered in chapters 9-19.

ORGANIZATIONAL PATTERN

Covered in chapters 20-26.

STRATEGY

The strategy statement is simply a detailed plan that explains one's overall lesson objective and the steps one intends to take in achieving that objective most efficiently and effectively. A well-written strategy statement benefits the writer of the lesson plan by helping to determine the best options to adopt when deciding on methodology, teaching techniques, interim objectives, and type and amount of proof and clarification support. It also helps anyone else who is tasked to teach or modify the lesson by explaining the rationale for choosing these options.

The strategy statement should be designed in such a way as to walk the instructor through the entire lesson, focusing on every element of the lesson. In this way, a comprehensive strategy statement helps the writer of the plan by forcing the writer to consider questions that are often taken for granted: (1) whether the overall lesson outline and order of main points and sub-points are the most logical and intuitively acceptable; (2) whether the teaching techniques one decides to use are the most appropriate for the lesson; and, (3) how much leeway one can take in the presentation before one changes the actual objective. Moreover, it provides a quick mental outline of the entire lesson that helps prevent the instructor's having to script, or slavishly rely on the lesson plan (thereby destroying the spontaneity of the presentation).

We suggest that you start by looking at your lesson objective and organizational pattern to decide on an overall strategic ordering of the main points. State this ordering up front; e.g., general to specific, specific to general, most to least important, known to unknown, simple to complex. This decision will give you a general focus to lead you toward the objective efficiently.

Follow this with a sequential statement of each main point and its associated sub-points to include method of presentation and rationales for the method and order of presentation. Each of these steps is important to help the lesson planner fit the elements together and consider all the factors necessary for justifying each decision. In effect, this method can be simplified by meticulously asking and answering the three questions that are indispensable for comprehensive lesson development: "WHAT, HOW, and WHY."

LESSON OUTLINE

To show the relative importance of lesson materials in the body of the lesson, an outline format is normally used. It is recommended that you use whatever outline protocol you are comfortable with.

CHAPTER 28

Teaching Plan

The teaching plan is divided into three main parts: introduction, body, and conclusion. The introduction will generally have three subparts: attention, motivation, and overview. The body will have the main points of the lesson as major subdivisions. The conclusion will have three subdivisions: summary, remotivation, and closure.

By the time we sit down to develop the teaching plan, several important steps in the planning process are already done. Lesson objectives and samples of behavior have been written. The subject has been extensively researched, a teaching method decided upon, a logical organization of the material has been selected, and a basic strategy for teaching has been documented.

The Teaching Plan is divided into three basic parts: Introduction, Body, and Conclusion.

INTRODUCTION

The introduction to a lesson should serve several purposes: to establish a common ground between the instructor and students, to capture and hold attention, to outline the lesson and relate it to the overall course, to point out benefits to the student, and to lead the student into the lesson content. While humor may be appropriate, the introduction should be free of irrelevant stories, jokes, or incidents that distract from the lesson objective. It should not contain long or apologetic remarks that are likely to dampen student interest in the lesson. There are three elements in the introduction of a lesson: gain attention, motivate, and provide an overview of lesson material.

Attention

To gain attention, the instructor may relate some incident that focuses on the subject and provides a background for the lesson. Another approach may be to make an unexpected or surprising statement or ask a question that relates the lesson to group needs. A rhetorical question (Have you ever...? or Can you imagine...?) may be effective. At other times, nothing more than a clear indication that the lesson has begun is sufficient. In all instances, the primary concern is to focus student attention on the subject.

Motivation

The instructor should use the motivation step to discuss specific reasons why the students need to learn whatever they are about to learn. In this motivational discussion, the instructor should make a personal appeal to students and reinforce their desire to learn. The appeal may relate the learning to career advancement or to some other need. But in every instance, the instructor should cite a specific application for student learning experiences. This motivational appeal should continue throughout the lesson. If a brief mention of needs is made only in the introduction, the instructor is "square-filling", not motivating.

Overview

The overview should provide an understanding of what is to be covered during the course. Effective visual aids can be helpful at this point. A clear overview can contribute greatly to a lesson by removing doubts in the minds of the learners about where the lesson is going and how they are going to get there. An overview may also include what will not be covered out and why. Students can be informed about how the ideas have been organized. In some cases lesson objectives are explained to the students. When objectives are communicated, use of the level of learning objectives, as written, may cause misunderstanding or confusion. In many instances, samples of behavior, slightly reworded, give the student a better understanding of the lesson objectives and the expectations on them. The better students understand what to expect in a lesson, the more they learn and retain. The purpose of the overview is to prepare students to listen to the body of the lesson.

It is not recommended that affective objectives or samples of behavior communicated. In most cases the knowledge that the instructor intends to change their beliefs and attitudes makes students less open to the level of influence the instructors wants to exert.

BODY

The body of the lesson goes here. This is where the "art" of training is applied. The material the instructor presents is included here. It may be in the form of bullets or in complete manuscript. Special notes to the instructor about conducting certain exercises, making non-verbal cues, asking specific questions, handing out materials, or displaying certain graphics should be included. This is the part of the instructor's guide that contains the most flexibility. This is done in whatever way works best for the instructor. Listed below are some other cues or reminders that the instructor might consider including in the body.

Transitions

Transitions are statements used by the instructor to move from the introduction to the body of the lecture, between main points, between sub-points within each main point, and from the body to the conclusion of the lecture. Transitions signal to the students that we are progressing to a new point, but they are also important in maintaining the continuity of the information being given. Consider this transition:

> We have discussed the precedents for a leadership development. Next we will consider the benefits of such a program.

This transition indicates a change in direction, but it does not indicate the reason for or importance of the change. For transitions to be effective, they should (1) mention the point just discussed, (2) relate that point to the objective, and (3) introduce the next point. Suppose the objective is for students to know the need for leadership development. Notice how all three steps are incorporated in the following transition:

> (1) We have discussed the precedents for a leadership development program, (2) but these precedents alone will not prove a need for such a program. To understand that need more fully, (3) we must next examine, in several practical situations, the benefits of leadership development.

When planned and used correctly, transitions contribute substantially to the continuity of the total lesson.

Interim Summaries

Summaries are useful tools for maintaining continuity within a lecture and for highlighting areas of particular importance. Summaries prepared for use between main points are not always necessary. In fact, if the point is very clear, a summary may be redundant and boring. You should use them, however, when main points are unusually long or contain complex or unfamiliar information. With summaries we repeat information concisely and reinforce student understanding before new information is presented. Summaries should not take the place of transitions. They should provide a means for us to progress logically from one main point through the transition and into the next point.

The summary given in the conclusion of the entire lesson should be designed so that it reviews for the students those facts or those aspects of a concept or principle that you consider particularly important. It may be helpful to think of this summary as a shortened version of the lesson itself, in which key ideas are related both to each other and to the lesson objectives.

Questions

Questions may be used to add continuity to the lesson. The instructor may plan rhetorical questions to use within a main point or in the conclusion of the lecture. Questions encourage students to review in their own minds the information that has been presented. They also indicate areas of special importance and should be phrased to allow students to see the relationship of these areas to the lesson objective. By asking both planned and spontaneous questions, the instructor can stimulate participation, emphasize important points and, perhaps most importantly, judge whether or not students understand the material.

Verbal Interaction

Whether verbal interaction is present at all, or to what degree it is used is a function of the teaching method being employed. When appropriate, verbal interaction takes place in two ways; students ask questions to clarify confusing points or to ensure their understanding of the information, and the instructor questions the students.

To be most effective, verbal interaction should occur consistently throughout the lesson. The instructor must allow ample time for discussion when planning and practicing the lesson. During the introduction, the instructor should encourage interaction. Students will be more likely to participate if the instructor indicates, through direct eye contact, frequent pauses, and a relaxed delivery, that student participation is welcome. Instructor questions are especially effective when they require students to summarize important information or to provide additional support in the form of personal examples.

Although frequent verbal interaction may be desired, it should not take priority over achievement of the lesson objectives. If a portion of the material is complex, unfamiliar to the students, or follows a necessary sequence, the questions may be distracting or cause confusion. In this case the instructor should ask students to hold their comments until after that material has been presented. This additional structure may also be necessary when time constraints do not allow student participation towards the end of the lesson. Careful planning is needed to ensure a comfortable balance between the material to be presented and the questions to be shared.

CONCLUSION

The conclusion of a lesson may stick with the students longer than anything else said. For this reason, we should give much care to its preparation. But the conclusion is also important in its own right. The conclusion of most lessons should accomplish three things: summarize, remotivate, and provide closure.

Summary

Short or interim summaries may be appropriate at various places in a lesson, for example, after each main point has been made. But final summaries come after all main points of the lesson have been made. An effective final summary retraces the important elements of the lesson. As the term suggests, a final summary reviews the main points in a concise manner. By reviewing the main points, it can aid students' retention of information and give them a chance to fill in missing information in their notes.

A final summary may require several minutes. While containing a brief restatement of significant information, it may require an expansion of key items to dependent upon the lessons objectives.

Remotivation

The purpose of the remotivation is to instill in students a desire to retain and use what they have learned. Effective instructors provide motivation throughout the lesson. But the remotivation step is the instructor's last chance to let students know why the information presented in the lesson is so important to the student as an individual. Perhaps it is important because it provides the groundwork for future lessons or because it will help do their current jobs more effectively. But whatever the reasons given, they should be ones that appeal directly to the students and show the importance to them of what was learned.

Closure

For many instructors the closure presents the most difficult challenge in planning a lesson. Students need to be released from active participation. In lectures they need to be released from listening. In interactive methods they need to know that it is time for their verbal participation to cease. Sometimes instructors, at a loss as how to close, say, "Well that's about all I have to say," or "I guess I don't have anything else." This type of closure is not very satisfying. There are much more effective ways of closing. Sometimes vocal inflection can signal that the lesson is ending. Quotations, stories, or humorous incidents can also provide effective closure. Sometimes when the lesson is to followed by others in the same block of instruction, we might say something such as, "Next time, then, we will continue with our discussion of…Between now and then if you have any questions, come to my office and I'll see if I can answer them for you."

AFTERWORD

I would like to close with a discussion I had with another training professional. When we discussed the basic premise for this book, he asked me if I thought Bloom and Krathwohl were dated. I took a moment to think about it and came to a conclusion.

While I do understand that these two theories were written in the 1950's. I believe they are every bit as relevant today as they ever were. Learning is popularly defined as a change in behavior based on instruction. If we accept this definition, then after receiving instruction, students should perform differently than before receiving it. Moreover, if we use student-centered level of learning objectives effectively, that behavior should be what we predicted it would be. We will be able to validate the students' success in learning by having them demonstrate the same physical or mental skill to the level described in the objective. Every decision you make should be directed towards each student attaining the learning objectives.

My closing question to my friend and it applies as well to each of you: How can you select the approach (i.e., method of instruction, organizational pattern, student exercises, etc.) until you know what you want the student to leave the training knowing or able to do?

ABOUT THE AUTHOR

Dan Chauncey received his B.S. from Wilmington College, Delaware, his M.A. in Human Resource Development and his MBA from Webster University in St. Louis, Missouri.

He currently works for Aon Management Consulting, in the process improvement and design practice area. He primarily consults and conducts training in Six Sigma methods for quality improvement.

Dan has worked in a variety of industries including insurance, healthcare, call centers, and energy. He also has also consulted in leadership development, change management, training design and delivery. He has facilitated more than 50 process improvement and process documentation teams, advised executive leaders in strategic planning, applied balanced scorecards, and developed numerous business processes particularly for service and healthcare environments.

He served as the Director of Process Improvement and Organizational Development for University Health System in San Antonio, Texas for several years. He developed and delivered courses in team development, quality tools and techniques, and statistical process control.

He also served for three years as Quality Improvement Manager for Humana, Inc. in San Antonio, Texas. Prior to public practice, Dan was the Director of Strategic Planning and Quality Improvement for the United States Air Force in San Antonio, Texas.

Dan lives in San Antonio, Texas with his wife Wanda and their daughter Rachael. When he is not working or writing, Dan loves riding his motorcycle with his wife around the Texas hill country.

APPENDIX A— THE CASE STUDY METHOD

The case method presents students with real life challenges. It helps bridge the gap in the classroom between theory and practice by applying previously learned concepts and principles. In the case study method students meet a simulated, real-life situation in the classroom in order to achieve an educational objective. The case study, typically written, is an account provided to students that serves as a basis for class activities and discussion. Usually, a case will describe a problem already faced by others in a given field. The greatest value of the case study is that it challenges students to apply what they know and comprehend to a realistic situation. The case method takes students out of the role of passive listeners and makes them partners with the instructor in applying the concepts and principles under study. The method enables students to think, reason, and employ data in a logical fashion, just as they will in a real job.

Variations of the case method were first used in teaching medicine and law, but over the years, the case method has been widely used in the study of business, management, and education. The method can be used in almost any learning area that can draw cases from real situations for study and discussion.

TEACHING VALUE AND LIMITATIONS

The case method is a flexible teaching approach. It can be the basis of an entire curriculum, a course, or simply an individual lesson. While the case method is versatile, there are times when other teaching methods are suggested in lieu of the case approach. The case method may not work with students who are immature, or with large classes. The method is not applicable in situations where students are learning a procedure or a single solution that has been accepted as "correct." Case studies do not lend themselves to development of objectives at the knowledge level, where the lecture and reading are usually more efficient. But once the knowledge level of learning has been achieved, the case study is an excellent way for students to progress to the higher levels.

A principle advantage of the case method is to provide students experience in solving problems. Many students can repeat isolated facts or principles, but they have difficulty in interrelating these facts and principles. The case method provides an opportunity for them to gain experience in making decisions and in working with other people. It exposes them to a number of different approaches to the solution of problems. As they learn various problem-solving techniques, they make their mistakes in the classroom and not on the job where an error is much more costly.

Students learn by encountering situations from real life instead of listening to lectures or reading theoretical descriptions of the solution to problems. By interacting with others, they learn to respect the opinions of others. Because the case may not list all pertinent facts, they also learn how to cope with ambiguity and uncertainty. As with real life, we sometimes ask questions and get answers, and at other times we can only ask questions.

TYPICAL CASE APPLICATIONS

Because of its versatility, the case lends itself to a wide variety of teaching conditions.

Case Courses

Some schools use the case method exclusively; especially graduate schools of business. The assumption is that the best way to prepare for a business career is to have experience in analyzing data and making decisions. Students in these courses are given complex cases to analyze and to solve. The quality of the analysis and the reasoning behind the suggested decisions are often more important than arriving at a single solution. In the classroom, students participate in collective analysis and decision-making. As more and more cases are analyzed, students begin to form generalizations that they can apply to new situations. Thus, case studies thus substitute for a period of on-the-job training.

Normally in the case study course, concepts and principles are not taught directly. Instead, they emerge gradually as students are forced to formulate theories to support their case decisions. Because these theories arise from practical work with problems, students remember them better and are able to recall them for similar solutions.

The case study course is usually conducted using group problem solving techniques in open class session. But the case may serve as an out-of-class written assignment, with students asked to bring solutions to class along with a rationale for their decisions. These solutions may form the basis for class discussion, and may also be turned in for the instructor to grade. A variation like this may overcome the need for relatively small classes in the pure case method.

While there are many instances where cases can be used in corporate training, I can't think of a better example than in leadership and management related lessons. Almost all of these lessons are designed for the higher levels of the cognitive domain, where the case is an excellent teaching method.

Capstone Method

A case or a series of cases is often used at the end of a body of instruction to help show the application of the course content. Often a course will proceed by lectures, discussions, and other more used methods. Towards the end of the instruction, students will apply what they have learned to a series of cases specifically designed to support the course objectives. This capstone method is particularly appropriate when students start at lower levels of learning (such as the knowledge level) and are brought gradually to the higher levels (such as the application level). The capstone method is particularly appropriate in leadership courses where readings and lectures might supply the basic material and case studies can allow an opportunity to practice the theory as a capstone experience.

The Short Case or "Problem."

The case also has applications at lower levels of learning. This technique is also called "use of the problem in teaching." A realistic problem situation, often a page or less in length, is used as a discussion vehicle. The instructor plans the lesson much like a guided discussion. For example, the objective of the lesson may be to have students comprehend the management principle of span of control. The instructor might introduce a situation in which a supervisor failed to take this principle into account. A serious accident or a dramatic event might then result.

The primary object is not to find a "correct" solution to the problem posed, but to understand the principles involved. The problem posed should be sufficiently interesting and difficult to involve all the class members for the time allotted. Because the written problem provides the discussion vehicle, the class can also be broken up into smaller discussion groups.

A variant of the short case can also be used when conducting group dynamics training where the emphasis is not on solving the problem, but on the interaction of group process. Similarly the short case can be used to demonstrate a decision making process, where the process is more important than the solution arrived at. A series of short cases or scenarios often works for reinforcing affective objectives, in human relations or equal opportunity exercises, for instance.

TYPES OF CASES

Teaching cases are situations from real life. There is no single format for cases, and great variation in the types of cases can be found. They may vary in length from a paragraph or two through many pages. For convenience sake, types of cases will be discussed in two categories: Case format and mode of presentation.

Full Text

A full text case contains all the information the student will need to deal with the situation and requires access to no other source. Business school cases, for instance, often illustrate a real situation faced by managers in the past. They contain the problem to be addressed, how the problem arose, the organization's structure, and the employees involved in the situation, as well as their perceptions at the time of the original incident. Cases of this type are usually of eight to fifteen pages, take considerable time to analyze, and are usually the basis of a case course. Students are required to read the case, perform an analysis, make a decision, and support that decision before their peers. With such a case the instructor is particularly interested in the student's ability to perform an analysis and make a decision.

Another full text case is the abbreviated case, which is much shorter, from one paragraph to several pages in length. An obvious consequence of the length is the diminished content. Since it is shorter, the focus is usually built in and the solution or solutions may be more limited. The abbreviated case may deal with one "problem," or it may define a scenario with a series of limited choices. The abbreviated case may lend itself to lower levels of learning.

A third variation of the full text case is the unsifted case. Although all the data required by students is presented at one time, it is given in an unorganized form, and extraneous information may be included. It is the student's task to select and arrange the information into some meaningful pattern for action.

Partial Text

With partial text cases students are given only limited information about the situation under study, and part of their job is to find or ask for the additional information they need for solution. In the incident-process case the instructor presents a brief incident, and the students are required to take some action, make a decision, or suggest recommendations. The instructor usually provides additional information only when the students request it; if it is not requested, it is not provided. Partial text cases are designed to teach students analysis and problem solving and also the ability to ask the right kinds of questions. The situation parallels real events because we often make decisions based on partial information. The incident-process case is designed to prepare students for this contingency.

In an interactive case students also receive limited information. Then they interact with other sources for additional data, return to class and ask for additional information or receive another segment of the case from the instructor, return to interaction, and so on. Other sources include additional readings, interviews, and library research. This process is similar to doing a research project. It is an artful blend of dealing with reality while, at the same time, acquiring additional knowledge and skills.

Like other partial text cases, the sequential case begins with limited information. The situation unfolds in succeeding installments of information to the students. At the end of each installment, students decide if intervention in the situation at that point is called for or not. Some incidents resolve themselves and intervention will only aggravate the situation. Other incidents continue to deteriorate and might even become irresolvable if intervention comes at an inappropriate time, or even too late. The sequential case is particularly suited for training in personnel management.

MODE OF PRESENTATION

Thus far, we have assumed that all cases are written. While the majority of cases do come in this format, other modes of presentation add variety, drama, and realism to the case class. Movies or videotapes can offer the participants the incident and the emotions of the case in a dramatic and lifelike way. Typically the film will unfold the situation to a decision point, then the students take over. After some individual or corporate decision has been made, the presentation can be continued by presenting more information, by using the outcome as an illustration and as a basis for further discussion, or for closure, whichever suits the student and instructor needs.

Moreover, videotape cases have the potential of increasing realism by presenting the original case participants who give their perceptions in their own words. How the original participants saw the case is often more critical and important to the student than the interpretations of these perceptions by a case writer. Another step toward case realism is to have a live presentation, where the participants come in person before the class to recreate the case experiences and respond to questions. A variation is to have students meet with the case participant, perhaps in the actual case environment.

CASE METHODOLOGY

More is required in teaching with the case method than simply reading the case and asking a few questions in class. Proper use of the case method requires conscientious preparation, presentation, and followup. As addressed in chapter 19, a high level of instructor knowledge is required to use the case method effectively.

Preparation

While there is no "best" way to approach case preparation, some generalizations can be made. The instructor should identify the specific learning objective toward which the class will proceed. Here, also, some appraisal of the relationship between the lesson and the rest of the curriculum is appropriate. Consider the instructor who has taught the principles of management to students in an earlier session; the objective now is to see if they can apply these principles to a given situation. Using the case in this way makes it a "capstone method," since the case reinforces and extends the teaching that has gone before.

Case Selection

In evaluating a case for use, regardless of source, we should ask ourselves five questions:

- Is it realistic? A case is realistic if it describes an actual problem or situation, even if the organization or participants are disguised. Obviously fabricated or fantasy cases are unlikely to have credibility. If the case is not realistic, it is hard to make the students' solution, decision, or action seem real. While it is theoretically possible to "invent" a case or use a composite of several situations, in practice such an approach is rarely as successful as dealing with an actual real-life case.

- Is it meaningful? The case should be meaningful to students so that they are able to identify with it in some way. They must be generally familiar with the problem either through their past experience or in the experiences they expect to face in the future. A case on a moonwalk, for instance, may not work for students who are not involved with space travel or who do not have the necessary technical background.

- Is it challenging? The case should contain actual or potential controversy. If the case is one in which the solution is obvious, it should be rejected.

- Is it complete? Usually a case is complete within itself. It presents enough information so that students can deal with the problems without reference to outside sources or the instructor.

- Does it provide for a logical difference of opinion? A case study that prompts a single line of analysis may not result in productive discussion. An acceptable case should provide an opportunity for reasonable people to differ rationally.

Case Writing

Quite often the instructor is unable to find the exact kind of case to achieve a specific objective. The solution may be to write a case to fit the specific need. The idea for a case may come in some current event, an article or periodical, or personal experience. For guidance in case writing, see *Teaching With Cases* by James A. Erskine, Michiel R. Leenders, and Louise A. Mauffette-Leenders, or *Case Research, Case Writing Process* by Michiel R. Leenders.

Writing the Teaching Note

A good case allows both the instructor and student to achieve educational objectives—the instructor to reinforce general principles with specific examples and the student to gain experience from the past in a close to real-life role. These objectives are both met by the instructor having analyzed the case beforehand in what is called a teaching note, which may include: Essential details in the case, major issues, analysis of these issues, evaluation of the case characters (their relationships, goals, values), prior knowledge students need to work the case, and questions to be included in the lesson plan which will guide the discussion.

The teaching note is not the solution to the case, but it should detail typical student activities that the case will stimulate and define the specific student outcomes the instructor expects. It should also define the level of student for which the case is written and relate the case to readings and to preceding or subsequent classes. The note should include at least an outline of the instructor's analysis of the case to show that it is internally consistent and able to hold up under analysis. After writing the teaching note, instructors will often find that the case contains insufficient or misleading information, and they may want to revise or amend it before giving the case to students. For certain groups, the case may assume knowledge of a process or background material that may need to be summarized in an attachment. A case on discrimination in promotion, for instance, may depend on a detailed knowledge of the promotion system and its appeals that the average supervisor may not have.

The instructor's preparation, then, should extend beyond the limits of the case to include political, economic, or social factors; policies and procedures in effect at the time of the case; and concepts and principles alluded to but not explained in the case. The more expert the instructors are about a case, the greater the chance of teaching it successfully, especially if the subject area is unfamiliar or the details skimpy. Once completed, the teaching note is included in the "body" section of the teaching plan.

Presentation

As with other aspects of the teaching case, there is no set procedure for conducting the class, but a number of general guidelines have worked well in past case sessions. The case method is inherently a student-centered approach. Keep instructor comments to a minimum and let the students do the talking.

Some case leaders begin with the question, "What is the issue here?", then go on to, "What are the pertinent facts?" Others begin with the more general question, "What action should be taken?" The approach depends on the intellectual maturity of the students and with the subject matter.

The case discussion is controlled much like the guided discussion, except that in the case, the instructor may enter the discussion more freely. The case instructor often keeps track of the discussion at the chalkboard or flipchart, so that the entire class has a visual record of where the discussion has been and where it is going. The questioning techniques used in case method are the same as for the guided discussion.

In case studies there is often no single right answer. It is more important to lead students toward sound application of principles than to persist in an endless search for one right answer. In the body of the lesson, the instructor should, of course, "guide" the discussion. But imposing the instructor's views on the students, passing judgments on contributions, and arguing, do little to encourage independent thinking or achieve the lesson objectives. Attempts to force a conclusion on the group often fail. Save instructor comments for the conclusion.

Case Roles

In the process of presenting a case, the instructor and students have roles they are responsible for. Fulfilling these roles increases the probability of a successful lesson.

Instructor Roles

As case leaders, how should we behave? We can dominate, control, and structure the discussion of a case and emerge from the discussion with our own solution. On the other hand, we can demonstrate a high degree of leadership skill in guiding and involving students in the discussion and solution of the case. In either instance, we serve in the role of recorder, questioner, and occasionally as clarifier or expert.

In the role of recorder, we provide direction and organization to the discussion of a case by writing ideas on a chalkboard or flipchart as the students submit them. We also record problem areas and items for further analysis and solutions by the discussion group. To avoid confusion or distraction, we might list the major elements of the selected decision or analysis process. Under each category, we might include specific student contributions. This task requires disciplined listening and undivided attention to every statement made during the discussion period.

One of the most important requirements of the case study method is the instructor's ability to use good questions. Questions are the principal device for clarifying contributions to the discussion and for relating ideas to the problem under discussion. Another questioning technique in the transfer of ideas is to review past experiences as they relate to a new problem. Frequently, to avoid student superficiality, a simple "why" question is used to confront a student's assertion and stimulate an orderly analysis of a problem. The instructor also has a responsibility to assure that the discussion is meaningful. We are the experts in teaching the subject and also in helping students express themselves. We should see that every student has an opportunity to participate. It is also our responsibility to establish rapport and maintain student interest in the case under discussion.

The Student's Role

The case method of instruction may require more student preparation than any other teaching method. If students do not prepare for class participation, they do themselves an injustice and deprive other students of possible discussion. As minimum preparation, they must read and study the case thoroughly. If there is time they might also refer to as many related references as possible.

During class discussion of the case, students should think reflectively and strive for cooperation rather than competition. They should share responsibility to contribute briefly and directly to the discussion and to assist in developing group concepts based on specific items of information. Thus, self-motivation is a significant element of the case study method, and this motivation obviously enhances the learning process.

Follow-up

What we do after the class session is over is often as important as what preceded the period. If student participation is expected, we should establish the criteria for assessing the participation beforehand, make it known to the students, and take notes while the impressions are still fresh in our minds. Even more important for future use of the case, we should review the lesson plan and note corrections needed in the case, possible changes in questions, and new lines of thought or different methods of analysis brought out by the students. In this way, the case stays fresh and becomes a more refined tool for use with subsequent classes.

SUMMARY

The case, properly used, initiates students into the ways of independent thought and responsible judgment. It faces them with situations that are not hypothetical, but real; it places them in the active role, open to criticism from all sides; it puts the burden of understanding and judgment upon them; and it gives them the stimulating opportunity to make contributions to learning.

In the problem-solving environment of the classroom, the students develop skills in communicating their ideas to others. At times, they may add to the ideas contributed by other members of the group, and, at other times, they may take exception to their peers' ideas. Both actions require effective communication techniques, and both involve a type of interaction that leads to consensus and understanding. The case study method increases the student's ability to appreciate other points of view, to explore and discuss differences of opinion, and, eventually, to reach an agreement. It forces students to think analytically, constructively, and creatively, and it gives them the satisfaction of participating in an orderly social relationship with others.

Appendix B—
Example of an Instructor's Guide

In Part VI we addressed the instructor's guide. Both the lesson and teaching plans were discussed and their purpose and contents explained. In an effort to provide an example, I have included an actual instructor's guide I developed and used to teach the use of metrics in a healthcare setting. While I do believe there is value in providing this example, I need to caution you use it as an example of the instructor's guide. Don't get caught up in the content.

METRICS LESSON PLAN

COGNITIVE LESSON OBJECTIVES:

The cognitive objective of this lesson is that each student be able to synthesize the applications of metrics and statistical process control in the improvement of processes with the elements discussed in this lesson.

Samples of Behavior:

- Each student will be able to define metrics and their relationship with the process improvement activities.
- Each student will be able to determine an appropriate metric for a given process.

- Each student will be able to define tampering and the associated risks.
- Each student will be able to interpret control charts as a basis for decision-making.
- Each student will be able to define and identify common cause variation.
- Each student will be able to define and identify special cause variation.
- Each student will be able to determine the type of data.
- Each student will be able to select an appropriate control chart.
- Each student will be able to explain the linkage between process control limits and process capability.

AFFECTIVE LESSON OBJECTIVES:

The affective objective of this lesson is that each student value the concept of statistical process control and process variation.

Samples of Behavior:

- Each student will openly promote the use of metrics as a management tool.
- Each student will associate tampering with poor process management.

LESSON DURATION:

- 8 hours

TEACHING METHOD:

- Guided discussion, case study, and simulation

STRATEGY:

- This lesson will follow a topical format. Each main point will contain student exercises that provide the student relevant examples and problems to ensure lesson objectives are being met. The first point will be to discuss metrics and how they are applied. Both the use of metrics and control charts as an ongoing process measure as well as using metrics and control charts internal to improvement activities. This point will establish a foundation of knowledge including the definition of a metric as well as a structured approach to design. The second point will address process variation and the appropriate actions depending on the type variation present as well as a discussion on tampering. The third point will provide the students with an understanding of the concepts of process capability. The Taguchi Loss Function will be touched upon as well as process capability and the concept of six sigma. The fourth point will be the use of control charts to graphically represent the metric display the metric as well as determine process stability. Students will learn how to identify the type of data (attribute or variable) and select an appropriate control chart. The charts (X Bar R, X Bar s, X MR, c, p, np, and u charts) will be discussed and applied, although student will not learn how to build these charts. The fifth point will focus on the interpretation of control charts. The course will conclude with an exercise that provides the students with an opportunity to run a process through the DMAIC and demonstrate how the use of quality tools and control charts can result in greater process knowledge and improved outcomes.

MAIN POINTS

Main Point I. Metric Overview

- Metric Definition
- Process Measure
- Process Analysis Tool
- Metric Description

Main Point II. Process Variation

- Types of Variation
- Tampering

Main Point III. Process Capability

- Taguchi Loss Function
- Process Capability

Main Point IV. Control Chart Selection

- Data Type

Main Point V. Control Chart Interpretation

- $\overline{X}$ R Chart
- $\overline{X}$ s Chart
- XmR Chart
- c Chart
- u Chart
- np Chart
- p Chart

Main Point VI. Process Improvement

- Process Improvement Capstone Exercise

METRICS TEACHING PLAN

INTRODUCTION:

Attention:

What is the mission of the University Health System?
> The mission of the University Health System is to provide, within the financial resources available, the highest quality care to our patients; to teach the next generation of health professionals; to advance medical knowledge and improve the delivery of patient care by supporting research; and to promote the good health of the community.

Motivation:

Is the part about "within the financial resources available" and "highest quality care" sometime at odds with each other? That is the what continuous improvement is all about. The use of metrics to measure our successes is a vital part of that improvement. We can reduce costs and improve patient care. We have to learn how to "keep score" in a manner that facilitates that.

For those of you who have had statistics before, it might help you, and it might not. Well, the use of control charts and the methodology Walter Shewhart developed may force you to look a little beyond those statistics paradigms. For the rest of you, don't despair. Statistics isn't rocket science, and we are only going to discuss the statistics that apply to statistical process control charts.

Remember, the most important thing you can do is ask questions. We are all here to learn. Your questions may well help another beside yourself. I know that I am constantly learning better ways to teach the material through your questions.

Overview:

Let's do a couple of things before we start:

- Introductions (include background in metrics or statistics)
- Student Activities
- Participating
- Expectations
    - By the end of the course each student will be able to define metrics.
    - By the end of the course each student will be able to determine an appropriate metric for a given process.
    - By the end of the course each student will be able to define tampering and the associated risks.
    - By the end of the course each student will be able to interpret control charts.
    - By the end of the course each student will be able to define and identify common cause variation.
    - By the end of the course each student will be able to define and identify special cause variation.
    - By the end of the course each student will be able to determine the type of data.
    - By the end of the course each student will be able to select an appropriate control chart.
    - By the end of the course each student will be able to explain the linkage between process control limits and process capability.

With these expectations you can see we have a lot of work to do if we want to. This course is going to address both theory and practice. Dr.

Deming said that true learning couldn't take place until you understand the theory.

Transition: Let's look at some of the new terms we will use.

Special Terminology

- $\bar{X}$—X means a variable and the bar symbolizes the average
- R or mR—R is the difference between the highest and lowest number in a series. mR is the difference between each subsequent data point.
- s—Standard deviation is a calculated number which shows the amount or variation within a set of numbers.
- UCL—Upper Control Limits
- LCL—Lower Control Limits
- Subgroup is the collection of units used to make up individual data points in a variables chart.

Transition: In order to meet our goals, we are going to move through this material in the following steps.

Course Outline

Main Point I. Metric Overview

- Metric Definition
- Process Measure
- Process Analysis Tool
- Metric Description

Main Point II. Process Variation

- Types of Variation
- Tampering

Main Point III. Process Capability
- Taguchi Loss Function
- Process Capability

Main Point IV. Control Chart Selection
- Data Type

Main Point V. Control Chart Interpretation
- $\overline{X}$ R Chart
- $\overline{X}$ s Chart
- XmR Chart
- c Chart
- u Chart
- np Chart
- p Chart

Main Point VI. Process Improvement
- Process Improvement Capstone Exercise

BODY:

Main Point I: Metric Overview

Metric Definition

a standard of measurement<no *metric* exists that can be applied directly to happiness>—Webster's Dictionary

In the past, organizations have often made decisions based on intuition and feelings. There is a place for intuition and feelings— but in an organization focused on process improvement, that place is as a compliment to data and facts. In process improvement, we are looking for *metrics* that can be applied directly to the process. When we measure processes there are two reasons or goals. One is to develop a metric that will quantify the "health" or success of the process (Process Measures). A "scorecard" if you will. The other is a short-term measure used to analyze processes (Process Analysis Tools).

Transition: Let's look at its use as a process measure first.

Process Measure

There are several ways to display data when it is used as a process measure. The key to determining what actions the graphic is intended to drive. For example, if the intent were to simply compare the current state to a desired state and then to initiate improvement efforts, either a static display that shows a comparison between the actual and desired states or a dynamic display would be appropriate.

A static display occurs when data is presented in tables, bar charts, or histograms. Static displays of data can be compared to taking a snapshot with a camera. Dynamic displays, on the other hand, are more like the moving picture obtained with a video camcorder. Each approach has its place and purpose. Your challenge is to know when to use each approach and understand the degree to which each type of display allows you to unlock the knowledge that is hiding inside the data. The best way to demonstrate these two approaches and the knowledge that can be gleaned from each one is by example.

Imagine that you are the manager of a family practice clinic. You have been collecting patient satisfaction surveys for the past 6 months and discovered one item that is consistently, the number one complaint—the wait time to see a physician. Your staff nurse tells you that the wait times do not seem very long. The employee who schedules appointments tells you, however, that the patients always seem bothered by the amount of time they have to wait to see a physician. So, what do you do with these two views of patient wait times? The correct answer is nothing!

What you should do is develop a process metric on patient wait time. You direct your staff to collect data on patient wait time, and after one week, you are ready to analyze the data. If you choose a static display approach to understanding variation, you would probably produce a tabular summary similar to that shown below:

Patient Wait Times—Week 1	
Number of Patients Seen	150
Average Wait Time	45 minutes
Goal	30 minutes

Or a graphical summary:

NOTE TO INSTRUCTOR:
Display Patient Wait Time Graphic

If you simply wanted to how the process is performing at a given point in time, both the table and the graphic would be adequate. If you want to improve it, however, they are both inadequate. The graphic display (histogram), gives you gain more insight than merely using numeric summaries, but you are still looking at data in a static fashion.

These static displays are suited to understand the current state and to drive improvement efforts, not to determine what improvements are appropriate. Most management decisions are based on static displays rather than on dynamic displays. Yet the processes managers are trying to understand are dynamic in nature, not static. An alternative approach would be to display the data using a dynamic display such as control charts.

Control charts are dynamic tool that graphically compares process performance data to statistically derived "control limits" drawn as limit lines on the chart. The prime use of the control chart is to detect assignable or special causes of variation in the process. The control chart distinguishes between common and special causes of variation through its application of control limits. They also help us understand process capability.

When the actual variation exceeds the control limits, it is a signal that special causes have affected the process and the process should be investigated. Variation within the control limits means that only "random" or common causes are present.

Interim Summary/Transition: The use of the control chart as a process metric allows you to make judgments about the process instead of simply understanding if it is meeting goals. It allows one to analyze a process.

Process Analysis Tool

Prior to action being taken on a, it should be determined if the process is being impacted by factors external to the process. This requires the use of a control chart. How to apply and interpret control charts will be explained later. In many cases, even when control charts are used as process metrics, addition data is required to improve the process. For example, in the case of patient wait times the process metric may be total patient wait time. In order to improve the process, you may develop control charts to show wait times at each step of the process (i.e., arrival to registration, registration to triage, triage to physician, etc). In either case the metric should be clearly documented.

Transition: Here is one way you can develop a standardized document.

Metric Description

A metric description consists of four parts:

- **Description:** The who, what, when, and how of the metric. It must be detailed enough to allow valid, repeatable, and consistent measurement to be made over time. The amount of detail required will vary from metric to metric, but at a minimum, it should consist of the following elements:
  - An unambiguous description of the metric
  - The population the metric will include
  - The frequency of measurement
  - The source of the data
  - Any equations required in doing the measurement
- **Target:** A desired expectation or goal. Whenever possible, this should be reflected as a range instead of a single measure. For example, a metric related to error rates may indicate an acceptable range of 1-2% average error rate; or a measure related to turnaround time might have a goal as an average turnaround time of 30-45 minutes.
- **Data Collection Method:** The how and when of collecting and recording of the data.
- **Presentation:** A description of the graphic presentation that will be used to display the data

Listed below is a format that works well when developing metrics. We will use this format throughout the class and recommend that you use it for your future metric development efforts.

Metric Descriptor	
Description:	
Target Range:	
Data Collection Method:	
Presentation:	

Customer Satisfaction Survey:

Rate the following statements on a scale of 1-5 with a rating of 1 signifying strong disagreement and a rating or 5 signifying a strong agreement.
- I am satisfied with the wait time during this visit.
- The staff members I interacted with were professional and courteous.
- Information was provided in a clear and understandable manner.

Survey Statement #1: *I am satisfied with the wait time during this visit.*	
Description:	Measures customer satisfaction with wait time in the UHC-D Medicine Clinic on a 5-point scale with 1 signifying strong disagreement and 5 signifying strong agreement. The data will be collected daily and serve as a process measure.
Target Range:	An average customer response of greater than 3.50.
Data Collection Method:	Statement #1 of a three-question survey given to customers at the conclusion of their visit. Data will be averaged daily. Each daily average will serve as a single data point
Presentation:	Since the data is measured on a Likert scale it is considered variables data. It was also concluded that each daily average constitutes a subgroup so there is one observation (the average) per subgroup. The XmR chart is selected.

Survey Statement #2: *The staff members I interacted with were professional and courteous.*	
Description:	Measures customer satisfaction with staff professionalism and courtesy in the UHC-D Medicine Clinic on a 5-point scale with 1 signifying strong disagreement and 5 signifying strong agreement. The data will be collected daily and serve as a process measure.
Target Range:	An average customer response of greater than 4.00.
Data Collection Method:	Statement #2 of a three-question survey given to customers at the conclusion of their visit. Data will be averaged daily. Each daily average will serve as a single data point
Presentation:	Since the data is measured on a Likert scale it is considered variables data. It was also concluded that each daily average constitutes a subgroup so there is one observation (the average) per subgroup. The XmR chart is selected.

Survey Statement #3: *Information was provided in a clear and understandable manner.*	
Description:	Measures customer satisfaction with communications clarity in the UHC-D Medicine Clinic on a 5-point scale with 1 signifying strong disagreement and 5 signifying strong agreement. The data will be collected daily and serve as a process measure.
Target Range:	An average customer response of greater than 4.00.
Data Collection Method:	Statement #3 of a three-question survey given to customers at the conclusion of their visit. Data will be averaged daily. Each daily average will serve as a single data point
Presentation:	Since the data is measured on a Likert scale it is considered variables data. It was also concluded that each daily average constitutes a subgroup so there is one observation (the average) per subgroup. The XmR chart is selected.

Metric Descriptor Development Exercise:

On the following page(s), develop at least one Metric Descriptor for a process you own or are associated with. Do not address the type of presentation. Take ten minutes to complete this exercise. After writing the descriptor, each student will share their metric with the class for discussion.

NOTE TO INSTRUCTOR:
Students should use blank metric descriptors in the student guide.

Main Point II: Process Variation

Simply reducing variation will usually decrease the number of dissatisfied customers. In most instances, it is easier and less expensive to reduce variation than it is to improve the output.

When the output of a process varies greatly, it is extremely difficult to initiate improvements in an efficient and quantifiable manner. Improvements in the output may be false readings which are really attributable to process variation. For example, you have a process with a great deal of variation. You decide on a process change that should improve the process average (e.g., a better score), after implementing, you notice that the next couple of periodic measures show that the score actually became worse. Naturally, you are inclined to revert to the original process. The problem is that the decrease may have been the result of the normally large amount of variation. In this instance, the work that went into developing the improvement may be wasted. The bottom line is that variation may mask true results of changes made to that process. The greater the variation, the greater the chance of misjudging improvements.

<u>*Types of Variation:*</u>

Common Cause:

Variation that is inherent to the process.

- **Stable Process:** A process that is in statistical control. There are no indicators of special cause variation present in the control chart. A stable process allows for prediction. When a process is stable there are two types of improvement which can take place:
    - **Improve:** We know that meeting customer requirements should be primary goal or target of a process. We also know that every process will contain variation. With this variation in mind, generally, the best way to quantify if we are on target is the average output or mean. Variation presents itself as outputs that are spread above and below the mean. By definition, an average generally results in approximately half of the outputs above the mean and half below. Variation that is on the negative side of the customer requirement naturally leads to customer dissatisfaction. Great stride can be gained in meeting customer requirements can be realized without even improving the process output.

Special Cause:

Variation that is external to the process. Special cause are identified by control charts when one or more of the following indicators are present:

NOTE TO INSTRUCTOR:
Display graphic of special cause control chart indicators.

- **Out of Control Process:** A process is considered out of control when special cause variation is present. When an out of control indicator is present, two actions should take place:
  - **Investigate:** When indicators of special cause variation are present, immediate action should be taken to identify the cause of the variation. If the cause cannot be identified, it must be considered a false reading and treated as common cause variation.
  - **Determine Appropriate Action:** Once the cause is identified, it must be determined if it is economically feasible to take action to preclude its recurrence or to reduce the impact of future occurrences.

Tampering:

Student Activity: Deming Funnel Experiment

NOTE TO INSTRUCTOR:
Conduct and debrief the Deming Funnel Experiment.

Listed below are the rules and discussion for each experiment cycle. Have students contribute additional examples.

Rule 1—No Compensation

Methodology: Do not adjust the funnel position. Center the funnel over the target and leave it there for the duration of the experiment.

Rationale: Intuitively, we know that this is probably not the way to get the best results. However, this strategy will give us some baseline data. We can compare the results using one of the other rules with this baseline to measure our improvement. We could also be lucky enough to hit the target once in awhile.

Business Analogy: Rule 1 gives us the best results without actually changing the process. The Funnel Experiment allows us to change the process by adjusting the height of the funnel. The lower the funnel, the less variation.

Other Examples:

NOTE TO INSTRUCTOR:
Have the students cite examples from the own experiences.

Rule 2—Exact Compensation

Methodology: Measure the distance from the last drop to the target. Compensate for the error by moving the funnel the same distance, but in the opposite direction.

Rationale: This rule attempts to compensate for the inaccuracy of the funnel. If the funnel drops the marble off the target by a certain amount, it is reasonable to suppose that moving the funnel in the opposite direction by the same amount will improve the results.

This rule requires us to remember the position of the funnel at the last drop.

Business Analogy: Rule 2 will actually increase variation. An example of Rule 2 in real life is adjusting a lathe after each piece to compensate for the difference between the diameter of the piece and the nominal specification.

Other Examples:

NOTE TO INSTRUCTOR:
Have the students cite examples from the own experiences.

Rule 3—Over-compensation

Methodology: Measure the distance from the last drop to the target. Center the funnel on the target, then move it the same distance from the target as the last drop, but in the opposite direction.

Rationale: In this case, we use the target as a basis for our adjustment, rather than the last position of the funnel, as in Rule 2. This is probably our only recourse if we know only the position of the target and the last drop, and not the position of the funnel.

Business Analogy: Rule 3 causes the process to explode in two directions. The result oscillates from one side of the target to the other. An example of Rule 3 in action is setting production targets for the current month based on last month's demand. The forecast for the current month is set to the actual demand for last month (analogous to resetting the funnel to the target position). Then the production plans are offset from the forecast: lower, if there is excess inventory, or higher, if there is a backlog (analogous to moving the funnel from the target).

Other Examples:

NOTE TO INSTRUCTOR:
Have the students cite examples from the own experiences.

Rule 4—Consistency

Methodology: Center the funnel over the last drop.

Rationale: The objective of Rule 4 is to maintain consistent results. Even if we miss the target, the results should be consistent, since we always aim for the position of the last drop. If we are off target, we can always take care of it later.

Business Analogy: Rule 4 also causes the process to explode. Eventually, the process output will wander off in a random direction, further and further from the target. A classic example of Rule 4 thinking is one worker training another, who then trains another, who trains another, and so on.

Other Examples:

NOTE TO INSTRUCTOR:
Have the students cite examples from the own experiences.

Transition: All of the strategies represented by rules 2, 3 and 4 amounts to tampering. Let's look the different types of tampering.

Tampering will always make matters worse. Of course, there are legitimate reasons for adjustments. If we allow the process to run without tampering, the results will tell us first, if the process is stable, and second, if the process average is offset from the target. Adjusting a stable process based the average will improve accuracy, but results will still vary. Top quality requires that variation be reduced. This can only happen when the process is understood, and changed based on this engineering knowledge. There are two types of tampering"

- **Type I Tampering: Treating common cause variation as special cause.**
- **Type II Tampering: Treating special cause variation as common cause.**

	Common Causes	Special Causes
Change and improve the process	APPROPRIATE ACTION Will improve performance	TYPE II TAMPERING Increases costs with no improvement
Find out what happened and prevent it from happening again, if possible	TYPE I TAMPERING Will increase variation and increase costs	APPROPRIATE ACTION Will improve performance

Student Activity: Determine Tampering

NOTE TO INSTRUCTOR:
You cannot determine if variation is special or common cause without using control charts, for the purpose of this exercise, we will infer the variation type from the narrative. The correct answer is underlined.

Exercise A: You have been collecting data on customer wait time in your pharmacy for several months. After several uneventful months, you begin receiving numerous customer complaints in one week regarding the wait time to receive their medications. Realizing that customer satisfaction is the goal, you establish a single line queuing system to route customers more evenly to your three service windows.

Type I Tampering
<u>Type II Tampering</u>
Not Tampering

Exercise B: You have been collecting data on customer wait time in your pharmacy for several months. Over those months, you have received several customer complaints regarding their wait time to receive their medications. Realizing that customer satisfaction is the goal, you apologize to each customer and immediately went to the service lines and began assisting customers to the most expedient service window.

<u>Type I Tampering</u>
Type II Tampering
Not Tampering

Exercise C: You have been collecting data on customer wait time in your pharmacy for several months. After several uneventful months, you begin receiving numerous customer complaints in one week regarding the wait time to receive their medications. Realizing that customer satisfaction is the goal, you realize that that week, several regular employees called in sick. You immediately contact the float pool supervisor establishes a method to replace absent employees on short notice.

Type I Tampering
Type II Tampering
<u>Not Tampering</u>

Main Point III: Process Capability

Process Capability: A measure of how well a process is currently behaving with respect to specification limits or targets.

NOTE TO INSTRUCTOR:
Display normal distribution graphic

The single, normal curve showed how the use of standard deviations allows us to determine the specific percentage of are under a given portion of the curve:

1 Standard Deviation = 68.26%
2 Standard Deviations = 95.46%
3 Standard Deviations = 99.73%

The set of double curves demonstrates that when the process mean is improved, the entire curve moves. It is important to remember that the mean is simply a measure of central tendency. The data points on both sides of the mean move proportionately.

Taguchi Loss Function:

NOTE TO INSTRUCTOR:
Display Taguchi Loss Function Graphic

The figure at the left depicts a traditional approach to quality: "Hit your target." As long as you are between your upper and lower target range you are doing good. As long as all the outputs are within the limits, one may say, "Our quality is perfect."

On the other hand, the figure on the right depicts the "Taguchi Loss Function" where cost increases as the process spread widens.

NOTE TO INSTRUCTOR:
Display Football Field Goal Graphic

Suppose you have two field goal kickers. Both kicker A and kicker B made 21 out of 21 field goals from 40 yards. Based on the results of each kick, which kicker would you want on your team?

Even though both kickers made all their kicks between the uprights (Upper and Lower Target Limits), Kicker A had less variation.

Process Capability

Since the process spread is a key factor in determining how well a process meets target, then a sensible measure should be the standard deviation. As discussed previously, the total process spread can be defined as 6 standard deviations (accounts for 99.73%).

NOTE TO INSTRUCTOR:
Display the specification limit graphic

If the specification or target width is equal to 6s, then process is capable of meeting specifications 99.73%. Conversely, if the specification or target width is less than the process width, the process is incrementally less capable.

The essence of the concept of process capability is that, since the process width is always 6s, the quality increases when the process specification or target limits are wider the control limits. When this occurs and, since any outputs that are outside the control limits are special cause, you can say that even when something external to the process happens that impacts the output, you can still meet customer requirements. For example, if the specification or target limits are +/- 6s (vs. the +/- 3s for the control limits) you would have an error rate of between 3.4 errors per million and 2 errors per billion depending on computational assumptions. Either way, the results are amazing.

In 1988, Motorola Corp. became one of the first companies to receive the Malcolm Baldrige National Quality Award. The award strives to identify those excellent firms that are worthy role models for other businesses. One of Motorola's innovations that attracted a great deal of attention was its Six Sigma program. Six Sigma is, basically, a process quality goal. As such, it falls into the category of a process capability technique.

The traditional quality paradigm defined a process as capable if the process's natural spread, plus and minus three sigma, was less than the engineering tolerance. Under the assumption of normality, this translates to a process yield of 00.27 percent. A later refinement considered the process location as well as its spread (C_{pk}) and tightened the minimum acceptable so that the process was at least four sigma from the nearest engineering requirement. A "Six Sigma Process" operates so that the nearest specification limits or engineering requirements are at least plus or minus six sigma from the process mean.

One of Motorola's most significant contributions was to change the discussion of quality from one where quality levels were measured in percentages (parts per hundred) to a discussion of parts per million or even parts per billion. Motorola correctly pointed out that modern technology was so complex that old ideas about acceptable quality levels were no longer acceptable.

Main Point IV: Chart Selection

Data Types

The first decision that needs to be made is whether the data are variable or attribute. Data are pieces of information that are generally gathered or obtained in some way. There are two type of data. Data are either variable or attribute. Variable data are things that are measured, whereas attribute data are things that are considered countable.

Variables data are collected through measurements, such as length, time, diameter, strength, weight, temperature, density, thickness, and height. One aspect of variables data is that you can decide the measurement's degree of accuracy. For example, you can measure an item to the nearest centimeter, millimeter, or thousandth of a millimeter. Data collected using a Likert or similar scale are considered variable data. Attributes data are data that can be classified and counted.

Student Activity: Determine Data Type

Example	Data Type (select one)
Number of delinquent medical records.	**Attribute** or Variable
Daily patient census.	**Attribute** or Variable
Patient accounts receivable balance.	Attribute or **Variable**
Patient cholesterol levels.	Attribute or **Variable**
Average length of stay.	Attribute or **Variable**
Difference between appointment time and arrival time.	Attribute or **Variable**
Completed history and physicals on the chart.	**Attribute** or Variable
Patient satisfied or not.	**Attribute** or Variable
Patient satisfaction on a 1-5 scale (Likert Scale).	Attribute or **Variable**
Average age of patients in a unit.	Attribute or **Variable**
Average salary level for hospital nursing staff.	Attribute or **Variable**
Patients with third party insurance.	**Attribute** or Variable
Time that a patient waits before seeing a physician.	Attribute or **Variable**

NOTE TO INSTRUCTOR:
Have students list three attribute and three variable examples of data that they work with.

1	Attribute
2	Attribute
3	Attribute
1	Variable
2	Variable
3	Variable

Variables Data:

Variables data are usually analyzed in pairs of charts that present data in terms of location or central tendency and spread. Location, usually the top chart, shows data in relation to the process average. It is presented in X-bar or X charts. Spread, usually the bottom chart, looks at piece-by-piece variation. Range (R), Sigma (s), and moving range charts are used to illustrate process spread. Run (SPC) and simple individuals charts can be used for any type of data.

$\bar{\bar{X}}$ R

$\bar{X}$ s

XmR

X bar and R Charts
X bar and R (range) charts are control charts that create a picture of a process over time. The X bar chart, on the top, shows the average or mean of each subgroup of data. The R or range chart, on the bottom, shows the range of each subgroup. When do you use X bar and R charts?

- When you want to see if your process is stable and predictable
- When you want to see how planned changes affects the process
- When the time order of the subgroups is preserved
- When you have collected data in subgroups larger than one but less than ten.

X bar and s Chart
X bar and s (standard deviation) charts are a variation of the X bar and R control chart. The X bar, usually on top, shows the average or mean of each subgroup of data. The lower chart shows the standard deviation of each subgroup. This chart combination is generally used when the when the subgroup size is large, for example, ten or more observations. When do you use X bar and s charts?
- When you want to see if your process is stable and predictable
- When you want to see how planned changes affects the process
- When the time order of the subgroups is preserved
- When you have collected data in subgroups is ten or more

X and Moving Range
Individuals (X) and Moving Range (MR) chart combination is a variation of the X bar and R control chart. It is used with subgroups containing one reading. The X chart, on top, shows each reading. The MR chart, on the bottom, creates ranges by finding the difference between consecutive readings. It uses absolute values, thus avoiding negative moving range values. When do you use individual and moving range charts?
- When you want to see if your process is stable and predictable
- When you want to see how planned changes affects the process
- When the time order of the subgroups is preserved
- When you have collected data with a subgroup size of one.
Note: Data may not be normally distributed (zone rules don't apply).

Attributes Data:

There are two types of attribute data: nonconforming and nonconformities.

- Nonconformities refer to defects or occurrences that should not be present but are. It also refers to any characteristics that should be present but are not. Dents, scratches, bubbles, and missing buttons are examples of nonconformities.

- Nonconforming Units are a count of defective units. It is often described as go/no go, pass/fail, or yes/no, since there are only two possible outcomes to any given check. It also refers to a count of defectives or rejects. For example, a light bulb either works or it does not. A project is either on time, or it is not. You can track either the number passing or the number failing.

There are four control charts for attributes data. For nonconforming units, there are p charts and np charts. For nonconformities, there are u charts and c charts. Run (SPC) and simple individuals charts can be used for any type of data.

- c Chart
- u Chart
- np Chart
- p Chart

c chart
C charts are a type of control chart that shows process changes over time by looking at the number of defects or nonconformities the process produces. For c charts, the subgroup size must be constant. C charts show the actual number of defects or nonconformities per subgroup. When do you use c charts?

- When you want to see if your process is stable and predictable
- When you want to see how planned changes affects the process
- When the data are a count of defectives or nonconformities
- When the time order of the subgroups is preserved
- When subgroup size is constant

u Charts

U charts show process changes over time by looking at the number of defects or nonconformities the process produces. The subgroup size can vary; therefore u charts show the number of defects or nonconformities in proportion to the subgroup size. When do you use u charts?

- When you want to see if your process is stable and predictable
- When you want to see how planned changes affects the process
- When the data are a count of defects or nonconformities
- When the time order of the subgroups is preserved
- When subgroup size can vary

np Chart

np charts are control charts that show how a process changes over time. They are used to monitor the number of defective or nonconforming units when the subgroup size is constant. For this reason, np charts show the actual number of defective or nonconforming units in each subgroup. When do you use np charts?

- When you want to see if your process is stable and predictable
- When you want to see how planned changes affects the process
- When you are counting defective or nonconforming units
- When the time order of the subgroups is preserved
- When subgroup size is constant

p Chart

P charts are control charts that show how a process changes over time. However, instead of using the actual count of defective or nonconforming units, p charts use a proportion of the defective or nonconforming units because the subgroup size may vary. When do you use p charts?

- When you want to see if your process is stable and predictable
- When you want to see how planned changes affects the process
- When you are counting defective or nonconforming units
- When the time order of the subgroups is preserved
- When subgroup size can vary

Control Chart Decision Matrix

	Variable Data	Attribute Data
Characteristics:	Continuous/ Measurable	Discreet/Countable
Chart:	$\overline{X}$ and R Chart: To chart measured data with a constant subgroup size less than 10 $\overline{X}$ and s Chart: To chart measured data with a subgroup size 10 or greater X and MR Chart: To chart measured data with a subgroup size of one	p Chart: To chart fraction defective with sample size constant or variable c Chart: To chart defects per units with constant sample size u Chart: To chart defects per unit with constant or variable sample size np Chart: To chart number of defective units with constant sample size

Control Chart Decision Tree

NOTE TO INSTRUCTOR:
Display and discuss control selection graphic

Student Activity: Determine Appropriate Control Chart

Based on the Metrics Descriptors listed below, determine the appropriate chart(s).

Metric Descriptor for Gathering Patient Information	
Description:	Measures amount of time required to collect vitals signs and pertinent information from patients in the UHC-D. Time is measured in whole minutes and is collected every day.
Target Range:	An average time of 4.0 to 5.0 minutes.
Data Collection Method:	Data is collected for the first patient to arrive after the start of an hour and half hour. Since the clinic operates 16 hours per day, the resultant sample size is 16. A time stamp is used to annotate start and completion time for each patient sampled.
Presentation:	

Answer: $\bar{X}$ and s charts

Metric Descriptor for Patient Falls	
Description:	The population included is the hospital-wide census. Counts the number of patient falls per bed day per week.
Target Range:	<.02 probability per patient bed day.
Data Collection Method:	The number of patient falls are recorded each time on a check sheet and compiled weekly against total bed days.
Presentation:	

Answer: u chart

Metric Descriptor for Lab Turnaround Time	
Description:	The metric indicates the amount of time, in minutes, from when the lab receives the request until the information is entered in the system. The population is all lab requests received from the emergency center.
Target Range:	≤ 25 minutes
Data Collection Method:	A sample size of five is used. Elapsed time from receipt to completion is captured by the system. At the end of each day, the total number lab requests completed will be determined, that number will be divided by 5, and the answer will be the count used to determine the sample. For example: 250 labs requests from the emergency center are completed each day, when divided by 5 the answer is 50. Cycle time for every 50th request will be included in the sample.
Presentation:	

Answer: $\bar{X}$ and r charts

Metric Descriptor for Errors in Dietary Errors	
Description:	The population includes all meals prepared for the pediatric inpatient unit. Data will be collected and charted daily. Errors will be based on differences between the patient dietary restrictions and the delivered meal.
Target Range:	The target is zero error. Not complying with meal restrictions may result in medical complications.
Data Collection Method:	As each meal is delivered, it is checked against the patient's dietary restrictions. Each error is indicated on a check sheet. The number of errors each day will be charted.
Presentation:	

Answer: c chart

Metric Descriptor for the Time Required to Complete an Abdominal Surgery	
Description:	The population includes abdominal surgeries. The time will begin when initial room preparation begins and ends when the patient departs the room.
Target Range:	Between 90 and 150 minutes
Data Collection Method:	Data is automatically captured by the scheduling system. Each surgery will constitute a single data point.
Presentation:	

Answer: X and mr charts

Metric Descriptor for Incorrectly Filed Documents	
Description:	The population includes all medical records returned. Counts the number of inpatient records with incorrectly filed documents. Errors are counted as the number of records with documents filed incorrectly.
Target Range:	<10% records containing incorrectly filed documents.
Data Collection Method:	As records are returned each day, every tenth record is selected for inspection. A check sheet is used to record the total number of records and the number of records with incorrectly filed documents.
Presentation:	

Answer: p chart

Metric Descriptor for Nonconforming Crash Carts	
Description:	All crash carts (20 carts) in UCCH are checked monthly against an approved checklist. Each cart must be appropriately stocked.
Target Range:	The goal is to have no cart improperly stocked.
Data Collection Method:	A list of all carts is maintained and all carts are checked once monthly at random times throughout the month.
Presentation:	

Answer: np chart

NOTE TO INSTUCTOR:
Once the students understand chart selection, move on to chart interpretation.

Main Point V Control Chart Interpretation

Student Activity: $\overline{X}$ R Chart Interpretation

Note: This is a student exercise. While the intent is to be as relevant as possible, the data used is not real.

Metric Descriptor for Lab Turnaround Time	
Description:	The metric indicates the amount of time, in minutes, from when the lab receives the request until the information is entered in the system. The population is all lab requests received from the emergency center.
Target Range:	≤ 25 minutes
Data Collection Method:	A sample size of five is used. Elapsed time from receipt to completion is captured by the system. At the end of each day, the total number lab requests completed will be determined, that number will be divided by 5, and the answer will be the count used to determine the sample. For example: 250 labs requests from the emergency center are completed each day, when divided by 5 the answer is 50. Cycle time for every 50th request will be included in the sample.
Presentation:	The data are variable. The subgroup size is 5, which is more than 1 and less than ten. The appropriate chart is the $\overline{X}$ R chart.

NOTE TO INSTUCTOR:
Students have data table and control chart available for review in the student guide.

Answer: While the mean is~24 minutes, the variation around the mean results in many of the patients waiting more than the 25 minute goal. Since the process appears to be stable, efforts should be initiated to decrease variation and improve the mean.

Student Activity #5: s Chart Interpretation

Note: This is a student exercise. While the intent is to be as relevant as possible, the data used is not real.

Metric Descriptor for Gathering Patient Information	
Description:	Measures amount of time required to collect vitals signs and pertinent information from patients in the UHC-D. Time is measured in whole minutes.
Target Range:	An average time of 4.0 to 5.0 minutes.
Data Collection Method:	Data is collected for the first patient to arrive after the start of an hour and half hour. A time stamp is used to annotate start and completion time for each patient sampled.
Presentation:	The data are variable. The subgroup size is 16, which is more than 9. The appropriate chart is the $\overline{X}$ s chart.

NOTE TO INSTUCTOR:
Students have data table and control chart available for review in the student guide.

Answer: The mean is above the goal of 4-5 minutes. Since the process appears to be in control, efforts should be initiated to reduce variation and improve the mean. It should be noted that while in many cases specifications for cycle time do not include a lower specification limit, this process does. It can be assumed that the customer requirements dictated that performing the process too quickly would be as negative as performing it too slowly.

Student Activity: XmR Chart Interpretation

Note: This is a student exercise. While the intent is to be as relevant as possible, the data used is not real.

Metric Descriptor for the Time Required to Complete an Abdominal Surgery	
Description:	The population includes abdominal surgeries. The time will begin when initial room preparation begins and ends when the patient departs the room.
Target:	≤ 150 minutes
Data Collection Method:	Data is automatically captured by the scheduling system. Each surgery will constitute a single data point.
Presentation:	The data are variable. The subgroup size is 1. The appropriate chart is the XmR chart.

NOTE TO INSTUCTOR:
Students have data table and control chart available for review in the student guide.

Answer: This chart shows a significant shift beginning at the nineteenth data point. At that point, that the control limits have been recalculated to indicate a change in the process. The new process is stable and well within specifications. Continue to monitor and take no additional action.

Student Activity: c Chart Interpretation

Note: This is a student exercise. While the intent is to be as relevant as possible, the data used is not real.

Metric Descriptor for Errors in Dietary Errors	
Description:	The population includes all meals prepared for the pediatric inpatient unit. Data will be collected and charted daily. Errors will be based on differences between the patient dietary restrictions and the delivered meal.
Target Range:	The target is zero error. Not complying with meal restrictions may result in medical complications.
Data Collection Method:	As each meal is delivered, it is checked against the patient's dietary restrictions. Each error is indicated on a check sheet. The number of errors each day will be charted.
Presentation:	The data are attribute. The count is of defects and the area of opportunity is equal since the census does not vary. The appropriate chart is the c chart.

NOTE TO INSTUCTOR:

Students have data table and control chart available for review in the student guide.

Answer: The last data point has spiked beyond the upper control limit. This indicates that special cause variation is present and should be investigated, and if warranted, action taken to preclude reoccurrence.

Student Activity: u Chart Interpretation

Note: This is a student exercise. While the intent is to be as relevant as possible, the data used is not real.

Metric Descriptor for Patient Falls	
Description:	The population included is the hospital-wide census. Counts the number of patient falls per bed day per week.
Target Range:	<.02 probability per patient bed day.
Data Collection Method:	The number of patient falls are recorded each time on a check sheet and compiled weekly against total bed days.
Presentation:	The data are attribute. The count is of defects and the area of opportunity is not constant since the census varies considerably. The appropriate chart is the u chart.

NOTE TO INSTUCTOR:
Students have data table and control chart available for review in the student guide.

Answer: The control chart shows while variation around the mean is low, it is not meeting the process goal. Since the process appears to be in control, efforts should be initiated to improve the mean.

Student Activity: np Chart Interpretation

Note: This is a student exercise. While the intent is to be as relevant as possible, the data used is not real.

Metric Descriptor for Nonconforming Crash Carts	
Description:	All crash carts (20 carts) are checked monthly against an approved checklist. Each cart must be appropriately stocked.
Target Range:	The goal is to have no cart improperly stocked.
Data Collection Method:	A list of all carts is maintained and all carts are checked once monthly at random times throughout the month.
Presentation:	The data are attribute. The count is for defective carts and the sample size remains constant at 20. The appropriate chart is the np chart.

NOTE TO INSTUCTOR:
Students have data table and control chart available for review in the student guide.

Answer: The last seven data points are above the mean. It appears that a process shift has taken place. This indicates special cause variation and should be investigated, and if warranted, action taken to preclude reoccurrence.

Student Activity: p Chart Interpretation

Note: This is a student exercise. While the intent is to be as relevant as possible, the data used is not real.

Metric Descriptor for Incorrectly Filed Documents	
Description:	The population includes all medical records returned. Counts the number of inpatient records with incorrectly filed documents. Errors are counted as the number of records with documents filed incorrectly.
Target Range:	<10% records containing incorrectly filed documents.
Data Collection Method:	As records are returned each day, every tenth record is selected for inspection. A check sheet is used to record the total number of records and the number of records with incorrectly filed documents.
Presentation:	The data are attribute. The count is of defectives and the sample size varies. The appropriate chart is the p chart.

NOTE TO INSTUCTOR:
Students have data table and control chart available for review in the student guide.

Answer: The last seven data points are below the mean. It appears that a process shift has taken place. Although the shift appears to have improved the process, it still indicates special cause variation and should be investigated, and if warranted, action taken to maintain the shift.

Main Point VI. Process Improvement

Successful process improvement requires making a clear distinction between product and process. Products may be characterized by conformance to specifications. Processes may be characterized by predictability. When combined, these two classification systems yield four possibilities for any process.

- Conforming and predictable—the ideal state
- Nonconforming and predictable—the threshold state
- Conforming yet unpredictable—the brink of chaos
- Nonconforming and unpredictable—the state of chaos

The ideal state occurs when a process is predictable and produces a conforming process. Such predictability in a process results from using Shewhart's charts to identify assignable causes in order to remove their effects. Product conformity results from having natural process limits (control limits) that fall within the specification limits.

How can a process achieve the ideal state? Only by satisfying four conditions:

- The process must remain inherently stable over time.
- The process must operate in a stable and consistent manner.
- The process average must be set at the proper level.
- The natural process spread must not exceed the product's specified tolerance.

Not satisfying any one of these conditions increases the risk of producing a nonconforming product. When a process fulfills these four conditions, then a consistently conforming product results. The only way to determine that these four conditions apply to your processes and subsequently are established and maintained day after day using Shewhart's charts.

Transition: Let's see if we can bring this all together with an exercise

Capstone Exercise

Student Activity—Catapult Experiment

NOTE TO INSTRUCTOR:
This exercise run requires each team be issued one catapult, one ball, and one measuring tape.

First Run Rules:

1. Each team will take one catapult, one ball, and one measuring tape. Each launching will be measured and annotated on the data collection sheet.

2. Every shot will be launched from a pullback angle of 177° and the peg settings should be as follows: A4; B3; and C3. Each person will per-

form as close to the same number of launches as possible in order to obtain 24 measures.

3. There will be a time limit of 15 seconds between successive launches. Each group will monitor their own times. Practice shots are not allowed.

4. Record each shot and once completed report the data to the instructor.

Objective: To fire the catapult and record the distance in inches for each of the launches. The measured distance will be from the back of the base of the launcher to the point where the ball hits the floor. The data will be recorded in the order they were obtained.

NOTE TO INSTRUCTOR:
Enter all data and create XmR control charts and walk the class through an analysis.

Have he students answer the following questions:

- Why was the XmR chart combination selected?
- What does the chart tell you about the variation?
- Do any process improvements that would reduce variation stand out as obvious?

NOTE TO INSTRUCTOR:
This exercise run requires each team be issued (in addition to the original materials) one roll or duct tape and one marker pen.

Transition: The next step is to reduce variation.

Each team should repeat the exercise. First taking 30 minutes to apply the DMAIC process (Define, Measure, Analyze, Improve, and Control) with the goal being to reduce variation.

NOTE TO INSTRUCTOR:
Explain to the students that the DMAIC process would usually take more than thirty minutes to work through. While the time is not realistic, it is simply intended to provide structure to their improvement session.

Second Run Rules:
1. Each team will take one catapult, one ball, and one measuring tape. Each launching will be measured and annotated on the data collection sheet.

2. Every shot will be launched from a pullback angle of 177° and the peg settings should be as follows: A4; B3; and C3. Each person will perform as close to the same number of launches as possible in order to obtain 24 measures.

3. Make process changes resulting from the improvement process. Changes are restricted by the materials handed out by the instructor. No other materials may be used. There will be a time limit of 15 seconds

between successive launches. Each group will monitor their own times. Practice shots are not allowed.

4. Record each shot and once completed report the data to the instructor.

NOTE TO INSTRUCTOR:
Enter all data from second run and display the new data using the original control limits.

Have he students answer the following questions:
- What did you notice after the first run?
- What did you notice about the control chart after the first run?
- What did you discuss during your improvement session?
- What changes did you implement?
- Were they all appropriate?
- What about the control limits after the process improvements?
- Is the process stable?
- Why not?

NOTE TO INSTRUCTOR:
Compute new control limits to show the process changes took place how the show the process shifted.

Have the students answer the following questions based on the new control limits:
- What does the chart tell you now?
- What would you do differently in a third run?
- Will this approach and measurement system work in your processes?

Transition: This exercise combines the almost elements

CONCLUSION:

Summary: Today we accomplished quite a bit. We have:
- Defined metrics
- Constructed metrics
- Learned about tampering
- Learned how to select and interpret control charts
- Learned to identify and understand variation (both common and special cause)
- Learned how to determine data type.

Remotivation: Now that you have a means to measure your processes and identify common and special cause variation, you are ready to improve processes with a greatly reduced risk of tampering. Using these tools will generally result in real, longer-lasting improvements.

Closure: Our plans are to present a "Quality Coach" course to people from the various departments. Our hope is that while this course establishes a baseline of knowledge, a more advanced course will result in a core team of "experts" to serve as internal consultants within their respective departments. If you are interested in becoming a "Quality Coach" contact me after the class and we can discuss the requirements.

INDEX

0-595-22783-X

Printed in the United States
44995LVS00003B/100